The Object Lessons series achieves something very close to magic: the books take ordinary—even banal—objects and animate them with a rich history of invention, political struggle, science, and popular mythology. Filled with fascinating details and conveyed in sharp, accessible prose, the books make the everyday world come to life. Be warned: once you've read a few of these, you'll start walking around your house, picking up random objects, and musing aloud: 'I wonder what the story is behind this thing?'"

Steven Johnson, author of *Where Good Ideas Come From* and *How We Got to Now*

Object Lessons describes themselves as 'short, beautiful books,' and to that, I'll say, amen. . . . If you read enough Object Lessons books, you'll fill your head with plenty of trivia to amaze and annoy your friends and loved ones—caution recommended on pontificating on the objects surrounding you. More importantly, though . . . they inspire us to take a second look at parts of the everyday that we've taken for granted. These are not so much lessons about the objects themselves, but opportunities for self-reflection and storytelling. They remind us that we are surrounded by a wondrous world, as long as we care to look."

John Warner, *The Chicago Tribune*

T0001508

OBJECTLESSONS

A book series about the hidden lives of ordinary things.

Series Editors:

Ian Bogost and Christopher Schaberg

In association with

BOOKS IN THE SERIES

Barcode

JORDAN FRITH

BLOOMSBURY ACADEMIC
NEW YORK • LONDON • OXFORD • NEW DELHI • SYDNEY

BLOOMSBURY ACADEMIC
Bloomsbury Publishing Inc
1385 Broadway, New York, NY 10018, USA
50 Bedford Square, London, WC1B 3DP, UK
29 Earlsfort Terrace, Dublin 2, Ireland

BLOOMSBURY, BLOOMSBURY ACADEMIC and the Diana logo are trademarks of
Bloomsbury Publishing Plc

First published in the United States of America 2024

Library of Congress Cataloging-in-Publication Data

Names: Frith, Jordan, author.
Title: Barcode / Jordan Frith.
Description: New York : Bloomsbury Academic, [2024] | Series: Object lessons | Includes
bibliographical references and index. | Summary: "arcodes are one of the most ignored yet
impactful objects of the last fifty years, and they have a much more interesting and
controversial history than most people realize"– Provided by publisher.
Identifiers: LCCN 2023014158 (print) | LCCN 2023014159 (ebook) |
ISBN 9781501399916 (paperback) | ISBN 9781501399930 (pdf) |
ISBN 9781501399923 (epub) | ISBN 9781501399947 (ebook other)
Subjects: LCSH: Bar coding–History. | Bar coding–Computer programs.
Classification: LCC HF5416 .F755 2024 (print) | LCC HF5416 (ebook) |
DDC 658.7–dc23/eng/20230515
LC record available at https://lccn.loc.gov/2023014158
LC ebook record available at https://lccn.loc.gov/2023014159

ISBN: PB: 978-1-5013-9991-6
ePDF: 978-1-5013-9993-0
eBook: 978-1-5013-9992-3

Series: Object Lessons

Typeset by Deanta Global Publishing Services, Chennai, India
Printed and bound in Great Britain

To find out more about our authors and books visit www.bloomsbury.com and sign up
for our newsletters.

To Stevie, my love and my support through everything

CONTENTS

IMAGES

1 THE LITTLE BLACK LINES THAT CHANGED THE WORLD

When I was sixteen years old, a friend of mine showed up to high school with a tattoo of a barcode on the back of her neck. I thought it was one of the coolest things I'd ever seen, and I asked her why she got a barcode tattoo. She responded vaguely with something about how we're all cogs in a capitalist machine, and my friends and I nodded in admiration. In a more romantic version of that story, I would tell you that was the moment I became interested in barcodes. But that's not this story. Instead, she put her long, blonde hair back down to cover her tattoo, I headed to class, and then I didn't spend more than a few seconds thinking about barcodes for almost twenty years. I interacted with barcodes countless times. I scanned groceries at self-checkouts and watched delivery people scan barcodes when they delivered packages. I used barcodes on tickets to board flights and to get into a bunch of indie-rock shows. Despite—or maybe because of—the fact that they were everywhere, I barely noticed barcodes. They were a part of the world I took almost completely for granted. It felt like they had always been everywhere, and to quote the popular podcaster Roman Mars, "It's hard to imagine now, a world without barcodes."[1]

The reality, of course, is that barcodes have not always existed. Some people reading this book may remember a time before most things they bought had a barcode. But for someone my age—I fall in the dreaded "geriatric millennial" category—it's difficult to remember a time before barcodes were key to everything from shopping to sending mail to getting into events. Until I started researching identification infrastructures a few years ago while writing a book about Radio Frequency Identification (RFID), I had never considered what a grocery store was like or how a supply chain was managed before almost everything had a barcode.[2] In other words, barcodes are a classic example of what happens when an infrastructural object becomes immensely successful: we stop thinking about it; it fades into the background. The learned invisibility and mundanity of the barcode is the ultimate symbol of its success.

Few technologies have been more successful. Barcodes were first patented in 1952, but the most recognizable barcode symbol—the IBM symbol used for the Universal Product Code (UPC) and International Article Number (EAN)— was not invented until the 1970s. Rather remarkably, that same barcode symbol remains almost completely unchanged as it now approaches its 50th birthday. Many of the major companies that helped develop the most significant barcode standards no longer exist, but those standards are still going strong. Essentially the same objects that transmitted data to early computers in the 1970s are now transmitting identification data stored in gigantic data centers. Some barcode technologies have changed, and some newer data standards for different types of barcodes have been developed. Nonetheless, the most iconic type of barcode that was used in the 1970s is still used today. There's something almost poetic about an infrastructural object remaining a steadfast constant as the systems it connects to became almost unrecognizable.

At almost fifty years-old, barcodes remain one of the world's most important data infrastructures. More than six billion barcodes are scanned every day, and there are few signs that number will decrease any time soon.[3] Of course, just because barcodes are everywhere doesn't automatically mean they're interesting. Pencils are everywhere, but not many people are writing books about pencils (though that might be a great book!). So why barcodes? Why write an entire book about objects that are basically just patterns of lines and spaces? The primary answer is because barcodes are one of the most important technologies of the last half century, and yet they are mostly ignored. As sociologist Nigel Thrift detailed in his cataloguing of transformative identification processes in the 20th century,

"The first of these is the humble barcode. The barcode is a crucial element in the history of the new way of the world, one which remains largely untold."[4] Barcodes played a significant role in everything from the rapid expansion of the global economy to the growth of logistics to the transformation of physical retail spaces. Decades before people started hyping "big data revolutions," barcodes were contributing to a data revolution of their own.[5] Just in the grocery industry, barcode adoption led to increased efficiency and inventory accuracy that enabled stores to stock more types of products and adjust inventory based on analyses of buying behavior.[6] Additionally, barcodes "transformed market research" by providing concrete data about consumer practices.[7] They even transformed physical spaces, and analysts have linked the growth of larger retail spaces to barcode adoption.[8]

While chapter 2 examines the early roots of barcodes in retail, their impact extended far beyond consumer spaces. Barcodes have long played an essential role in global supply chains and made it possible to track products at an unprecedented scale. By the early 1980s, the defense and automotive industries adopted barcodes to manage supply chains, and many other industries followed soon after. By 2004, 90% of all Fortune 500 companies used barcodes in some aspect of their business.[9] To return to the earlier quote from Nigel Thrift, the sheer scale of the contemporary global economy would be difficult to imagine if barcodes did not exist—the identification data they produce is a key enabler of global markets that require a huge amount of information to manage complex logistics. As MIT professor Sanjay Sharma argued, "If barcodes hadn't been invented the entire layout and architecture of commerce would have been different. The impacts are very difficult to overestimate."[10] Yet despite the crucial role barcodes have played in the contemporary way of the world, their story remains mostly untold.

The other reason I want to tell the story of the barcode is that it's a far more interesting story than most people might imagine. The success of barcodes was far from inevitable, and their future was in serious doubt at a few moments of juncture. In an article that belongs in the pantheon of "this did not age well," *Business Week* declared in 1976 that the barcode was a failure just two years after it was adopted in the grocery industry.[11] The barcode's story is filled with twists and turns, consumer protests, and labor battles about automation. Barcodes even became a symbol of the possible apocalypse in some evangelical Christian communities and managed to play a significant role in the 1992 US presidential election. Beginning in the 1980s, the same barcodes people scan on cans of soup became a prominent symbol used in dystopian science fiction and are even a popular tattoo people still inscribe on their bodies. This book examines how a technology initially adopted for grocery stores somehow became an iconic symbol of capitalism and one of the most recognizable objects in the world.

The many symbols of the barcode

Barcodes are one of many technologies grouped under the automatic identification and data capture (AIDC) umbrella. Other AIDC technologies include radio frequency identification (RFID), optical character recognition, magnetic stripes, facial recognition, and smart cards—all of which automate processes of identification in one way or another. Barcodes are certainly not the most powerful AIDC technology. As discussed in chapters 2 and 3, they work by containing identification data in patterns of lines and spaces, and the amount of identification data they're able to contain cannot compete with AIDC technologies like RFID. In addition, barcodes are optical technologies that must be scanned through a direct line of site, which contrasts with more advanced wireless AIDC technologies that have broader communicative potential. Nevertheless, while they may not be the most powerful identification infrastructure, barcodes have been by far the most successful. Decades before people started talking about communicative objects as part of the Internet of Things, barcodes had already become a bridge between the physical and digital that made material objects machine readable and connected them to digital networks. No other infrastructure in history has automated more identification data than the humble barcode.

While barcodes fall under the larger AIDC umbrella, barcodes themselves are also an umbrella term for many different symbols. The most recognizable symbol is the IBM barcode that is used in retail all over the world and found on the cover of this book. That barcode symbol is likely what most people think of when they hear the word "barcodes," but it's merely one of almost 300 different types of barcode symbols in existence.[12] Most barcode symbols are barely (if ever) used, but there are various symbols—such as Code 39, Codabar, and Code 128— that have been widely adopted in various industries. Many of those symbols look a lot like the iconic IBM symbol, with the main difference being how much data they contain within their varying patterns of lines and spaces. In fact, the most famous barcode symbol happens to be one of the least powerful in terms of data capacity. The IBM symbol contains only 12 digits, which are far fewer than symbols like Code 39 that can encode 43 numbers and letters. The simplicity of the IBM barcode, as I discuss later, ended up being one of its strengths.

To complicate things a bit more, not only is the word "barcode" a term for a wide range of symbols, but there are also two broad categories of barcode technology. Barcodes like the IBM symbol or Code 39 are examples of "linear barcodes," which means the data is contained in one direction and the symbol is one dimensional. Linear barcodes are the lines and spaces most people think about if they ever think about barcodes at all. However, as chapter 8 examines, in the 1990s a different type of barcode technology emerged: 2D barcodes, the most recognizable of which is the QR Code. I'll leave the details of how 2D barcodes work for later, but the most important point is that many people might not realize 2D barcodes even *are* barcodes. They work in fundamentally the same way as linear barcodes by encoding data in patterns and spaces, but they don't typically contain the recognizable lines of linear barcodes.

I promise the rest of this book is not going to be about lists of AIDC technologies or catalogs of different barcode symbols. I address those points in this introductory chapter primarily to explain choices made in the rest of the book. Throughout the following chapters, I mention different types of barcodes, but for clarity's sake, most of the discussion focuses on UPC/EAN barcodes because those were the first widely adopted barcode and paved the way for other symbols used in other industries. The oldest of all the widely used symbols is also still the most famous and is the type of barcode that almost everyone reading this book would recognize. Additionally, throughout this book, when I use the word "barcode" I'm mostly referring to the more traditional types of linear barcodes unless otherwise noted. In chapters 8 and 9 I do use the phrase "linear barcode" to compare them to 2D barcodes, but unless the context dictates, you can assume that when I write "barcodes" I'm talking about linear barcodes rather than their 2D cousins. I made that decision for a very practical reason: I use the word "barcode" a whole lot throughout these chapters and figured this book would be much easier to read if I used one word rather than two whenever possible.

Maybe most importantly, I wanted to note early on that barcodes aren't just the lines on products at grocery stores. They're also the patterned objects identifying movement in supply chains, the mobile boarding passes scanned to board planes, the multiple symbols on the packages left on your doorstep, and the QR Codes scanned to do everything from access a restaurant menu to get video instructions for an at-home Covid-19 test. Barcodes are everywhere, and they come in many shapes and sizes.

Conclusion

I first started researching barcodes as a hobby, as a side project to distract from other work. That hobby turned into something more as I immersed myself in the history of this most humble of objects. I went from casually reading about barcodes to spending a week in the summer of 2022 at Stony Brook University's George Goldberg archive combing through primary sources key to the barcode's history (and yes, I was surprised to discover that there's an entire archive devoted to the barcode). I found something almost romantic about these objects that hold so many parts of our world together while almost never getting the credit they deserve. I initially assumed there would never be enough to write more than a few short articles about barcodes and ended up struggling over which stories I had to cut from this book. Immersing myself so deeply in the world of the barcode has been—and no one was more surprised by this than me—the most fulfilling research journey of my career. Ultimately, if this book accomplishes what I hope, you'll stop for just a moment the next time you're in a self-checkout line and think about all the history and deeper cultural meaning embedded in those ubiquitous patterns of lines and spaces.

2 HOW WE ALMOST ENDED UP WITH A BULLSEYE BARCODE

When objects become old enough and mundane enough, it can feel like they arrived on the world stage ready-made. Barcodes—at least for me—were one of those objects. They felt like they were everywhere for as long as I could remember, and they were so immediately recognizable and so taken-for-granted that I didn't think twice about them. I never considered the antecedent technologies that helped lay the groundwork for the retail I spaces I grew up with, and it never occurred to me that the barcode came very close to looking drastically different.

Beginning the story of the barcode involves making a somewhat arbitrary decision about a starting point, which is true for pretty much any object's history. I want to start with two 19th century technologies—the cash register and the punch card—invented decades before the barcode was even a glimmer of an idea in an early patent application.

The first cash register was developed in 1879 by a man named James Ritty who created a prototype primarily to stop employees from stealing from his businesses. Before the cash register, retail checkout ran mostly on an honor system. Employers had to trust that their employees were charging the correct amount, and records were rarely kept about prices charged. In stepped Ritty with his device that could record price inputs and produce records that could later be checked for fraud. Just in case you had any doubt about Ritty's goals, he named his device "The Incorruptible Cashier."[1]

Ritty struggled to profit from his invention, and John H. Patterson bought his business in 1884. Patterson renamed the company National Cash Register (NCR), which still exists today and was the manufacturer of the laser scanner used to read the first ever UPC barcode ninety years later. Whereas Ritty had struggled to capitalize on his "Incorruptible Cashier," Patterson turned the cash register into a staple of retail. Much of the marketing Patterson used to do so was, to put it mildly, not very subtle. To quote an early NCR pamphlet,

> I am the oldest criminal in history
> I have acted in my present capacity for many thousands of years.
> I have been entrusted with millions of dollars.
> I have lost a great deal of this money . . .
> I am the OPEN CASH DRAWER.[2]

Cash registers were designed from the start to reduce the chance of human error—whether intentional or not—and record pricing inputs to remove some human agency from the checkout process. What cash registers could not do was automate data collection. People still had to manually type prices into registers, and early marketing didn't focus much on improving efficiency. Consequently, while the invention of cash registers was an initial step towards limiting human error in the retail system, tracing the roots of data automation the barcode would later build upon requires another transformative 19th-century technology: the punch card.

The US Constitution mandates that a national census must be conducted every ten years to collect data about the population. By the late 19th century, population growth had made the census process unmanageable. The main problem was not collecting data; it was tabulating the data. In the leadup to the 1890 census, the overwhelming scale of data entry had reached a boiling point, and some commentators predicted that inputting the 1890 census data wouldn't be completed until it was time for the next census.[3] To address that problem, the US government held a contest asking for proposed fixes, a contest won by a man named Herman Hollerith. His solution? The electro-mechanical Hollerith Tabulator.

The system Hollerith developed relied on what became a major technology for much of the twentieth century: the punch card. People could input census data by punching holes in a card that could then be automatically read by

Hollerith's machine. By some estimates, the use of punch cards and the Hollerith Tabulator led to a tenfold increase in the amount of data that could be inputted in a single day. Punch card technologies were then adopted by various industries, and as management professor Joanne Yates notes, "By the early decades of the twentieth century, the devices were being widely discussed in the business and trade press . . . and interest in and adoption of such tabulating systems grew among large firms in a variety of industries."[4]

Punch cards remained an enduring data infrastructure for many decades and were a crucial technology in the early days of computing. They remained such an important data infrastructure that they were even a key part of the Space Race. For example, in the movie *Hidden Figures* about the important role Black women played in the 1960s US space program, the mathematician Dorothy Vaughn (played by Octavia Spencer) takes a book from the "Whites Only" section of the library. She takes the book to teach herself the programming language Fortran, which in the 1960s required people to enter data into mainframe computers by inserting punch cards. While punch cards mostly became obsolete as a data storage medium by the mid-1970s, they still survive today in some election systems.

Punch card systems impacted a wide variety of industries but were not an ideal fit for retail industries that needed to track individual item data on a massive scale. Cash registers, on the other hand, impacted retail practices but did little to automate data entry. Consequently, people—especially in the grocery industry—began searching for ways to automate item-level data entry in retail as early as the 1930s.[5] The grocery industry would have to wait decades to settle on a solution: the barcode.

The invention of the barcode

The creation of the barcode can be traced back to a fortuitously overheard conversation in the late 1940s. As the story goes, a graduate student named Bernard Silver overheard a grocery store executive pitch Drexel University faculty on the idea of an automated supermarket checkout. The faculty members weren't interested, but Silver was intrigued and mentioned the conversation to another graduate student named Joseph Woodland. The two men began brainstorming ideas but struggled to develop a viable solution, and Woodland left Drexel University not long after. Luckily for Woodland, he went to stay with his grandparents in Miami, Florida, where he spent days hanging out at the beach. It was on one of those beach days on a random January morning when, in a story Woodland acknowledged "sounds like a fairy tale," he had a flash of inspiration.[6] He was sitting on the sand and thinking about the dots and dashes of Morse Code and drew four lines in the sand. He looked at the lines and realized that, instead of dots and dashes, people could use lines of varying width to communicate data. Those ephemeral lines in the sand were the inspiration for the most ubiquitous identification infrastructure ever invented.

Woodland brought his idea to Silver, and the two men applied for a patent in October 1949 with the rather generic title of *Classifying Apparatus and Method* (the word "barcode" did not exist yet). The patent was granted in 1952, and the symbol displayed on the opening page of the patent was the first ever barcode. As Woodland and Silver stated in the patent, the symbols "provide [an] automatic apparatus for classifying things according to photo-response to lines and/or colors which constitute classification instructions and which have been attached to, imprinted upon or caused to represent the things being classified." Rather presciently, their patent also notes that while "one application of the invention is in the so-called 'super-market' field . . . it should not be considered that the invention is limited to that field only."[7] It was indeed the grocery industry that led the way on barcodes, but barcodes eventually spread to countless industries in ways Woodland and Silver could never have imagined.

One element immediately stands out in Woodland and Silver's patent: the barcode symbol on the first page looks nothing like the barcode symbols found everywhere today. Rather than the vertical lines and spaces that hundreds of millions of people have scanned countless times, the barcode symbol Woodland and Silver created was a series of concentric circles emanating outward in the shape of a bullseye. The bullseye they created followed the same principles as the objects that were eventually scanned hundreds of billions of times, but the data was contained in circular lines rather than the vertical lines of later barcode symbols. That bullseye barcode was more than just a historical footnote buried in the pages of a patent. The world came very close to ending up with bullseye barcodes rather than the vertical black lines that eventually became iconic.

While the barcode was first patented in 1952, it took decades—and the invention of other technologies—before the technology was widely adopted. Woodland and Silver knew they had created something useful, but throughout the 1950s they struggled to make their case. Woodland began working at IBM in 1951, and he tried to convince IBM to invest in his invention but was told his barcode was too futuristic and needed more powerful data processing systems than existed at the time. A company named Philco bought the patent in 1962 and sold it to RCA in the mid-1960s. Tragically, Bernard Silver would never see what the object that he helped invent would become. He died in 1963 at the age of 38, more than a decade before the barcode was adopted in the grocery industry.

A few years before Silver's tragic death, the pieces that eventually made barcode systems possible started falling into place. Computing power had continued to improve, but even more importantly, Theodore H. Maiman built the first working laser in 1960. Lasers are used in a wide range of applications, but one of the laser's most important (yet unsung) contributions comes from the role they played in transforming barcodes into a viable identification technology. Before lasers, there was no fast and accurate way to retrieve the data stored in the patterned lines of barcode symbols. The invention of laser technology was a key addition to the network the barcode needed to become the defining identification infrastructure of the 20th century.

By the late 1960s, laser-powered optical scanners were commercially available and the first major attempt to adopt barcode technology was underway. That first attempt—the KarTrak system— was championed by the railroad industry. KarTrak used a color-coded barcode symbol to automatically identify railcars as they passed by fixed scanners, and the North American railroad industry mandated the use of KarTrak barcodes in 1967. However, there's a reason why the barcode on the cover of this book is one you'd find at a grocery store and not a multi-colored barcode attached to a rail car: despite the industry-wide mandate, the KarTrak project never took off and was abandoned in 1977. KarTrak became almost a footnote in the barcode's story that would soon be overshadowed by one of the most successful industry collaborations in history: the grocery industry's collaboration on the Universal Product Code (UPC).

The creation of the Universal Product Code (UPC)

By the late 1960s, it became clear that something needed to change in the grocery industries in the United States and Western Europe. Some members of the grocery industry had dreamed of ways to automate checkout and inventory as early as the 1930s, but little progress had been made on that front. The barcode, along with laser-powered optical readers and more affordable computing power, finally offered a possible solution, a solution that only became more urgent as retail labor costs skyrocketed throughout the 1960s.[8] By the latter half of that decade, companies like RCA and Carecogn had begun conducting pilot tests in grocery stores to assess the viability of their barcode systems.

While the grocery industry hoped barcode systems could help cut labor costs, the implementation of barcodes faced significant hurdles. Industry executives decided early on that barcode systems would only be viable if basically every relevant part of the industry—including the stores, manufacturers, printers, packagers, and distributors—all agreed on one data standard and one symbol.[9] If one grocery chain decided to use one barcode symbol and another chose a different symbol, the entire project would fall apart. After all, installing barcode systems was going to cost a massive amount of money (estimates expected it would cost about $200,000 to install barcode systems in a single grocery store).[10] If everything wasn't standardized and packagers and manufacturers had to put different codes on products to ship them to different stores, the system was a non-starter. The process would cost far too much money, solve too few problems, and never get off the ground.

The grocery industry met the challenge in the age-old way large organizations have confronted problems: they formed a committee. The committee—tantalizingly named the Ad Hoc Committee—was composed of representatives from across the grocery industry, including supermarket owners, packagers, and manufacturers. The committee was tasked with analyzing the feasibility of barcode systems, and if they decided the project was feasible, figuring out how it would all work.

The Ad Hoc Committee, as detailed in Stephen Brown's (who was the general counsel for the committee) excellent book about this early period of barcode history, made decisions that significantly shaped the next five decades of identification practices across multiple industries.[11] The first decision they made was that barcodes were a viable option for grocery stores. That was the easiest part. The next two major steps took years and created a system that remains mostly unchanged almost fifty years later. The first step involved creating a data standard that could be adopted by the entire grocery industry. Standards may seem boring, but they're crucial to so many parts of our lives, and barcodes would be little more than random lines and spaces without the standards that determine the organization of the data they contain. Without agreed-upon data standards, barcodes wouldn't really matter. The committee decided early on that the process of creating a data standard had to remain separate from the process of choosing a barcode symbol, a point emphasized in a confidential report created in the early 1970s.[12]

The standard the committee created was called the Universal Product Code (UPC), which is now referred to as the UPC-A to differentiate it from related UPC standards that were later developed. The UPC-A consists of 12 digits, and the next chapter explains how those digits work to identify products. But taking a higher-level view, the most important decision focused on what the committee wanted the barcode to do. Many barcode data standards work as "license plate" codes, a precedent established by the UPC and still in wide usage today. License plate codes are intentionally simple: all they contain is a string of numbers that feed into a database to identify an object. A UPC-A barcode (and most barcodes for that matter) doesn't contain actual data about an object. There's nothing in a UPC-A barcode about prices, weight, point of origin, or anything like that.[13] The numbers in a UPC-A simply link to a database record that contains more detailed product records. The decision to make the UPC standard intentionally simple influenced much of the next 50 years of barcode development.

The third major decision was maybe the most dramatic: deciding which barcode symbol to choose. For that process, the Ad Hoc Committee created a subcommittee called the Symbol Selection Committee that first met on March 31, 1971. That committee then determined requirements for the barcode symbol and asked companies to submit proposals. The final choice involved intense debate and came down to the committee's final meeting exactly two years later.

Barcodes are objects that contain patterns of lines and spaces that can be translated into data; nothing about a barcode requires it to be a series of straight black lines.

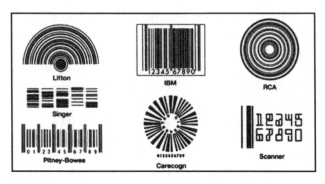

IMAGE 1 The seven finalists chosen by the Symbol Selection Committee "Confidential Draft: Choice of a Universal Product Code," 54.

Woodland and Silver's initial barcode pattern was in the shape of a bullseye and didn't have straight lines at all. To decide on a symbol, the committee solicited proposals and ended up with seven finalists (see image 1). Many of the symbol finalists—including the RCA "bullseye," Litton's "fan," and Carecogn's "sun"—barely resemble the barcode symbol that is still ubiquitous a half-century later.

The final decision on the symbol was not an easy one, and the committee was still undecided heading into their final two meetings in March 1973. In those meetings, the committee "achieved a consensus that the fundamental choice was between the bullseye symbol proposed by RCA and Litton, and the oversquare proposal of IBM."[14] In an interesting twist, Joseph Woodland—the co-inventor of the barcode himself—played a role in the symbol selection decision. More than two decades earlier, Woodland had invented the bullseye code RCA submitted for consideration, but he was working for IBM in the 1970s and coauthored a report that made the case for the symbol his colleague George Laurier had invented less than a year earlier.[15] Woodland's advocacy for his colleague's invention over his own played a role in persuading the committee as the final decision came down to the wire.[16]

If you've been to a grocery store in the last few decades, you know that the committee chose the IBM symbol, but just how close we came to ending up with an entirely different barcode is mostly lost to history. RCA threatened the committee by saying that the company would drop out of the barcode market if the bullseye barcode was not chosen, and there was significant worry that "by opting for the oversquare symbol instead of the bulls-eye, the Committee may have dramatically slowed the pace of implementation."[17] The committee members chose the IBM symbol despite those worries, and at that point the Ad Hoc Committee's work was mostly complete: they had developed the UPC data standard and chosen a barcode symbol, and I doubt even the most optimistic members of the committee could have imagined that both would remain mostly unchanged a half-century later. The committee's work also established guidelines that were adapted a few years later in Europe when the equivalent European committee went through a similar process. The European committee chose the same IBM symbol and developed their own data standard—the International Article Number (EAN), now known as the EAN-13 to differentiate it from related EAN standards—that was almost identical to the UPC standard except for one additional digit to identify the country of origin. With the symbol in place and the data standard established, the barcode was ready to deploy.

The grocery industry and beyond

On June 26, 1974, the first product with an official UPC barcode— a pack of Wrigley's gum—was scanned at a grocery store in Troy, Ohio. The event received some coverage in a handful newspapers, but nothing too significant. The significance of that pack of gum only became clear in retrospect as, after an initial period of disappointment and doubt, barcodes eventually spread throughout the world.

Many years later, the Smithsonian Museum in Washington, DC added a facsimile of that pack of gum and one of the first barcode scanners to its permanent collection. When I think about one of the world's most famous museums adding a pack of gum to their collection, what strikes me is how many moving parts needed to fall into place to arrive at that moment. Joseph Woodland had to visit that Florida beach and file his patent with Bernard Silver; the laser had to be invented in 1960 and computing infrastructure had to become more powerful. The grocery industry had to work together in one of the largest-scale examples of industry cooperation that didn't involve governmental backing.[18] Rival grocery stores, manufacturers, packagers, printers, and so on had to buy into a system and agree upon what a series of 12 digits should mean and what symbol should contain those digits. At so many points, the entire project could have failed, and we might not have had barcodes at all.

The primary documents I found from those now mostly forgotten Ad Hoc Committee meetings showed that the committee members felt like they were working on something important. However, nothing I came across in my archival work suggested that anyone had any idea just how important their work would become. In fact, the "developers of the UPC believed that there would be fewer than 10,000 companies, almost all in the US grocery industry, who would ever use the UPC."[19] More than a million companies now use the UPC in one way or another, and the UPC later inspired a wide range of barcode standards. In other words, the barcode succeeded beyond the wildest dreams of its early proponents, and that committee decided on an object that would eventually become one of most iconic symbols of capitalism. Think about that for a moment . . . these meetings were focused on the *grocery industry*. A group of executives interested in partially automating grocery store checkouts set in motion a string of events that impacted everything from the growth of the global economy to how militaries manage supply chains to people's tattoo choices. And it all happened with little fanfare. As two Harvard business professors later noted, "Even the strongest advocates for the UPC did not foresee fully what they were unleashing."[20]

The spread of the barcode to other industries did not happen immediately after the grocery industry formalized the UPC. As covered in the next chapter, the early years of the UPC barcode were tumultuous and the project came dangerously close to failing altogether. However, by the early 1980s adoption of UPC barcode technology had begun to increase significantly, and as a 1984 journal article explained, "the success of the UPC has encouraged many related applications" in other industries.[21] Two of those industries were especially important for establishing the barcode as the world's dominant identification infrastructure: the defense industry and the automotive industry.[22]

In the late 1970s, the US Department of Defense (DOD) launched the LOGMARS project to address the growing logistical problems the industry was facing with identifying and tracking objects in the ballooning military industrial complex. The push to develop LOGMARS was influenced by the grocery industry's success, but the DOD faced challenges that differed from the inventory needs of retail. After years of planning, LOGMARS determined that they needed more data capacity than was possible with the IBM symbol adopted for the UPC. LOGMARS chose the Code 39 barcode symbol, which was similar to the design of the IBM symbol but could contain 43 alpha-numeric characters. By encouraging suppliers to the US DOD (it's almost unfathomable just how big the US defense industry is) to begin barcoding items, the project played a major role in establishing the viability of barcode technology in logistical supply chains.

Around the same time as the LOGMARS project was launched, the automotive industry began a major project to standardize barcode usage. The industry had been an early adopter of barcodes, but the system was basically the Wild West and quickly becoming unworkable. Competing car companies and car parts manufacturers had begun using barcodes without any standardization, and by 1980, there were more than 50 barcode symbols and data standards in use. The lack of standardization was costing companies a huge amount of money and the systems often weren't interoperable. Consequently, the Automotive Industry Action Group (AIAG), inspired by the cooperation in the grocery industry a decade earlier, spent years developing an industry-wide data standard that used the same Code 39 symbol as the LOGMARS system. As one automotive executive described the project, it was "the gamble that started a revolution," and it was a gamble that paid off handsomely as manufacturers bought into the new standardized barcode system that was formalized in 1983.[23] At that point, three of the largest industries in the US had put their faith in barcode technology, which had ripple effects as barcodes then spread throughout the global economy.

LOGMARS and the AIAG standardization owed a significant debt to the work initially done by the Ad Hoc Committee in the early 1970s. While they created different data standards and adopted a different barcode symbol, the core structures of the system were based on the groundwork laid by the UPC. Both systems also chose the Code 39 symbol that uses the vertical lines and spaces model that closely resembles the IBM symbol adopted for the UPC. In fact, almost all widely adopted linear barcode symbols—for example, the Code 128 and Codabar symbols—use similar line patterning to the IBM symbol chosen by the Ad Hoc Committee. If that committee had made a different choice, it's possible that other industries might have followed their lead when they had to decide on their own barcode symbols. So many of the auto-identification practices developed over the last fifty years can be traced back to those Ad Hoc Committee meetings and the choice of a symbol that is now an icon— for better or worse—of capitalism and globalization. I'm not sure a bullseye would have held the same weight.

3 AN EARLY BRIDGE BETWEEN THE DIGITAL AND THE PHYSICAL

In the fifty years since the creation of the UPC, so many technologies have been developed that would be unrecognizable to someone in the 1970s. The Internet barely existed, mobile phones were still decades away from widespread adoption, phrases like "cloud computing" would have sounded like science fiction jargon, and the idea that billions of objects would communicate as part of something called the "Internet of Things" would have sounded like nonsense. Barcodes, on the other hand, have remained mostly unchanged and yet are more omnipresent than ever.[1] Even with the rapid rise of networked objects in the Internet of Things, barcodes remain the most common bridge between physical objects and digital information.

The Internet of Things refers to the development of communicative objects—ranging from networked cars to implanted microchips to Wi-Fi enabled toasters—that merge the digital and physical in novel ways.[2] Much of the hype about the Internet of Things focuses on newer technologies like 5G infrastructure, Wi-Fi, and Bluetooth for connecting objects to broader networks. However, long before anyone started talking about the Internet of Things— even long before most people started talking about the Internet—barcodes were laying the groundwork for linking physical objects to digital information. Barcodes were the most important antecedent technology for today's Internet of Things and occupy a somewhat strange place in the contemporary data landscape: they are simultaneously the most important precursor for flashier, newer technologies that connect objects in novel ways while remaining the most common way those connections are made possible.

Barcodes were the first widely adopted technology that transformed the movement of physical objects into digital data. They are, as architects Hiromi Hosoya and Markus Schaefer argue, "bit structures" that are "the mechanism by which the virtual establishes its logic in the real," and the UPC is the "thumbprint of a good by which its identity is asserted in the realm of information."[3] Long before academics began theorizing about hybrid spaces and mixed realities that merge the digital and physical in new ways, barcodes were already creating hybrid environments as mediators that bridged the physical world and the digital. For as novel as the

Internet of Things might seem—and some parts of the vision are undoubtedly new—the idea of transforming objects into digital/physical hybrids didn't begin in the 21st century; it began with the humble barcode.

Pointing out that barcodes were an early bridge between the physical and digital raises a significant question: namely, how does any of that work? It's fairly clear how objects can become more communicative by connecting to 5G or Wi-Fi networks. What is less clear is how a bunch of vertical lines work as the "bit structures" that make material objects machine readable.[4] Additionally, a major part of the power of barcodes is that we don't *need* to understand how they work to interact with them. People don't need to know what those black lines are doing when they check out at a grocery store or scan a ticket to get into an event. Most of the time barcodes just work and don't demand our attention. Drawing from Geoffrey C. Bowker's call for an infrastructural imagination that involves exploring how the infrastructures that surround us function, this chapter examines *how* barcodes transform objects into data.[5] To understand the barcode's role as a bridge between the physical and digital, it's first necessary to explain how that bridge is built.

Reading between the lines

At a basic level, barcode symbols are patterns of lines (typically black, though they don't have to be) and spaces that contain data. The data contained in those lines can be read directly by scanners, which is how barcodes make objects optically readable by larger systems, a process I'll explore in more detail by explaining how the most recognizable of all barcode symbols works: the IBM symbol used for the UPC and EAN standards.

Image 2 is a UPC-A barcode, which is the same barcode you'd find if you walked to your pantry and took out a box of cereal or a bag of flour. This particular type of barcode consists of fifteen pairs of black lines and white spaces printed over a string of numbers. The printed numbers are a redundancy built into the system and don't need to be there for the barcode to work, but they're mandated by the UPC and EAN standards so that a cashier can manually input the numbers if the barcode is damaged. If the scanner can read the barcode, the magic happens in the space between those lines.

The identification data is contained in those pairs of lines, but here it gets a bit more complicated: the UPC-A standard only contains twelve digits, so three of those line

IMAGE 2 A standard UPC-A barcode (published under a Creative Commons license).

pairings don't contain any data. Instead, on the left, middle, and right of the barcode are three longer pairs of lines called "guard bars" that tell the scanner when to start and stop (alternatively, if you listen to certain sources, they might mark people as followers of the Antichrist, but you'll have to wait until chapter 6 for that part of the story). The actual identification happens in the other twelve pairs of lines, each of which uses a binary process to represent a digit between zero and nine.[6] The digit is determined by two factors: the thickness of each line in the pair and the amount of space between the lines. The coding is binary because the scanner determines the data by reading for the 1s of the black lines and the 0s of the white spaces, and thicker black lines read as multiple 1s in the decoding process.

The patterns of lines and spaces used to represent zero through nine are tightly standardized, so every single line pairing that contains a four, for example, is the same. Because the line patterns are standardized, if someone wanted to, they could train themselves to decipher the numbers in a UPC-A or EAN-13 barcode by memorizing the line patterns used to represent each number. In a sign that I maybe got a bit too into my research, I'll admit I spent a few hours figuring out how to read the pairs of lines in a UPC-A barcode.[7] EAN-13 barcodes add one more step because they contain an extra digit to mark the country of origin. The barcode symbol is identical to the UPC and contains the same number of lines, so the European organizing body had to get creative to fit a thirteenth digit. They solved that problem by creating a math equation that uses the other twelve digits to calculate the thirteenth digit, which allowed for identifying countries of origin while also making sure that EANs and UPC were interoperable.

The same basic process is used for most linear barcode symbols that, despite some differences, use patterns of lines and spaces to contain data that turns physical objects into machine-readable, digital-physical hybrids. The patterns of those lines enact "the virtual in the real" by connecting physical objects to digital records through strings of identification numbers.[8] Their role as a machine-readable "bridge" is why barcodes are the most important antecedent technology to the contemporary Internet of Things. The barcode itself is only one part of the story, however, and a series of numbers contained in patterns of lines doesn't mean much on its own. To understand how the barcode became the most omnipresent link between material objects and digital systems, we need to turn to the most exciting part of any transformative technology: bureaucracy.

Data doesn't speak for itself

The ability to transmit data contained in patterns of lines is part of what make barcodes one of history's most successful data infrastructures, but scanning a barcode is only the most visible step in a much larger process comprised of standards documents, administration, registration fees, and global organizations. On their own barcodes are just containers of data, and a significant amount of work is required to make data meaningful.[9] If barcodes are a bridge between the digital and physical, without multiple layers of deeper infrastructural work they'd be a bridge to nowhere.

Infrastructures are mostly designed not to be noticed, and tend to only "become visible upon breakdown."[10] Barcodes themselves are an example of that dynamic. They're obviously not literally invisible, but people rarely pay attention to them except when they won't scan. Infrastructures often become even more invisible as one digs deeper into a system. After all, infrastructures that support higher-level practices are often shaped by lower-level infrastructures, which themselves are shaped by even lower levels of infrastructure. Sociologist Susan Leigh Star described the dynamic more concisely than I ever could when she argued that "it's infrastructure all the way down."[11] The deep infrastructural layering includes the "hard" infrastructures of material objects and the "soft" infrastructures of various forms of buried social organization.[12] The barcode as a material object is an example of "hard" infrastructure, but barcodes are significant actors in dispersed global networks because of the layers of discursive and bureaucratic "soft" infrastructure that become embedded within communicative objects moving throughout the world.

To examine those deeper layers of infrastructural work, I will continue to focus on the UPC-A and EAN-13, though almost every widely used barcode standard is supported by similar structures. As discussed earlier, a UPC-A barcode contains twelve digits used to identify an object. On their own, those twelve digits aren't impactful without the infrastructures in place to make them meaningful. If manufacturers or stores could use whichever twelve numbers they wanted to identify an object, the whole system would quickly fall apart. The reason people can scan barcodes at grocery stores without knowing anything about how they work is largely because of a not-for-profit organization called GS1.

GS1 is a global organization that was formed when the Universal Code Council (which governed the UPC) and the European Article Numbering Association (which governed the EAN) merged. GS1 is a standards organization that dictates how different technologies and data structures must be implemented. Many of the organization's standards focus on barcodes—both linear and 2D—though they also manage standards for other AIDC technologies like RFID. And while there are many standards organizations that impact numerous aspects of our lives, GS1's standards are the single "most widely used system of standards in the world."[13]

GS1 is the bureaucratic infrastructure that makes global barcode systems possible, and companies must pay GS1 to be assigned a manufacturer code. That GS1-assigned manufacturer code is required to operate in the global UPC and EAN network, and GS1's bureaucratic control makes sure that each manufacturer code is unique to avoid overlap between products. In addition, GS1 provides strict directives about what each digit in a UPC or EAN barcode must signify. That standardization of barcode data might not seem exciting, but it's an essential part of the identification process. Without a standards body like GS1, cashiers would likely still be manually inputting prices.

To illustrate how the data standardization works in practice, I'll take the numbers from the UPC-A code for a 32-ounce package of Riviana arborio rice that happened to be the first thing I grabbed from my pantry:

074401 *91041* 1

Those first six digits in bold are the manufacturer code assigned through GS1. Manufacturer codes can range from 6-10 digits depending on how many individual products the company produces. A company that only makes one product might only need a 10-digit manufacturer code, whereas companies that make many products requires a shorter manufacturer code so they can use the other digits to identify their individual products. In the case of the arborio rice, the next 5 digits in italics are the individual product code assigned by the manufacturer.[14] The product codes are required to be specific for identification purposes: a 32oz container of Riviana arborio rice has a different identification code than a 16oz container, and a two-pack of 32oz arborio rice would have yet another unique identification number. The final digit is what's called a "check digit," which is calculated through a mathematical formula to make sure that the numbers in the UPC are accurate.[15] With an EAN barcode, the process is the same except it includes a mathematical formula to add a thirteenth digit at the beginning of the code to denote the manufacturer's country of origin. The country codes are also determined by GS1 and its 116 local member organizations.[16]

While this section has explained how the numbers in a UPC-A or EAN barcode work, maybe the key takeaway is that very few people *need* to know any of that information. The clearest sign of the success of GS1 as a bureaucratic infrastructure is that most people have no idea the organization exists. The standards documents, teams of administrators, registration processes, and organizational structures are all examples of the invisibility of "soft" infrastructure. Unless the system breaks down, the infrastructural work of organizations like GS1 remains invisible, even as these bureaucratic structures hold entire global systems together. Embracing an infrastructural imagination involves more than just understanding the materiality of the lines and spaces of the barcode; it also involves examining underlying structures that make the billions of barcodes moving through the world identifiable.

Back to the future (of the Internet of Things)

With the growth of the Internet in the 1990s, much academic theory and popular discourse conceptualized the digital as a separate "cyberspace" disconnected from the objects and people that make up our physical spaces.[17] John Perry Barlow's 1996 cyberspace manifesto, for example, famously declared that the digital was "the home of the mind," separate from the physical world "where bodies live."[18] However, more recently the conceptualization of the digital and physical as distinct and separate has lost much of its luster. People have mostly turned away from the cleaving of the two and instead are examining how the digital and physical have become increasingly intertwined. As many people have argued in one form or another, we increasingly move through hybrid spaces where physical processes are reliant and essentially inseparable from streams of digital information.[19] People access information about nearby places through smartphone screens; many physical spaces often won't operate as intended without various layers of software. And obviously, just as the physical world is shaped by the digital, there is no digital without extensive physical infrastructure built over many decades. The connected objects of the Internet of Things have only made that hybridity even clearer. Many material objects now have communicative, digital, affordances that link them to both other objects and human bodies. Hybridity is our present, and hybridity will be our future.

Barcodes are rarely included in discussions of the hybridity of contemporary life. Instead, most of the focus falls on relatively newer technologies like smartphones, augmented reality displays, and networked objects. Nonetheless, long before refrigerators had Wi-Fi connections or smartphones displayed location information, barcodes were already merging the physical and digital at an unprecedented scale. Barcodes were the Internet of Things before the Internet; they were the bridge between a world of mobile objects and digital records. In other words, barcodes were making spaces hybrid long before hybridity was cool.

People don't have to know how the binary patterns of barcodes contain data linked to digital records; they don't have to know anything about the organizations that do the work to make that data meaningful. They can scan barcodes countless times without a second thought, and that learned invisibility is a part of the power and beauty of infrastructure. These infrastructures—and it truly is infrastructure all the way down —are designed to be ignored. Embracing an infrastructural imagination means looking closely at the objects and systems we're not meant to spend time thinking about. In the case of the barcode, it means both deciphering the lines on the material objects and acknowledging how deeper infrastructural work becomes buried in those lines to make barcodes so impactful.

Barcodes as metaphorical bridges are built on binary patterns of lines and spaces that make objects machine readable. On a conceptual level, that machine readability gives objects a "voice" and enables them to communicate with larger systems. That "voice" might not be very loud and might not be able to say much more than strings of identification numbers, but objects become communicative, nonetheless. The concept of the Internet of Things focuses on creating objects that can communicate, and the lines and spaces of the barcode laid the groundwork for the more powerful affordances of newer wireless technologies like Bluetooth and RFID. In an alternative reality in which barcodes hadn't established the viability of networking billions of objects, we might not have the contemporary push for the Internet of Things at all.

Just as importantly, the barcode's global infrastructures illuminate how much invisible work goes into making objects communicative. Barcodes have become one of the most consequential data infrastructures in history because of the human labor to standardize data structures, administer identification numbers, and exert control to ensure interoperability. This same process is just as important to a networked car as it is to the barcode. In other words, the history of the barcode shows that giving objects communicative, nonhuman agency requires a significant amount of human work. Beneath the surface of whatever the Internet of Things eventually becomes will be layers of bureaucracy and administration, many pages of standards documents, and large organizations responsible for holding it all together.[20] We can only hope those processes are nearly as seamless as the vast barcode systems that are still going strong many decades since they were created.

4 CONSUMER PROTESTS, LABOR RIGHTS, AND AUTOMATION

Part of the power of barcodes comes from their learned invisibility. They're everywhere, and as with other omnipresent technologies, it can feel like they've *always* been everywhere. The barcode's mundanity, however, was hard-earned. Before barcodes became accepted—and mostly ignored—objects of everyday life, they were greeted by significant protests in the 1970s that almost changed the course of history. The protests arose again in the 1990s, and the controversies and concerns feel almost as relevant today as they were decades ago, with concerns about financial transparency, automation, and labor sparking resistance and protest. These problems continue to arise as the media technology landscape keeps shifting.

Learned invisibility is one of the defining features of infrastructure, and barcodes have certainly earned that invisibility over five decades.[1] Nevertheless, infrastructures are not always invisible, and as anthropologist Brian Larkin argued, they often go through moments of hypervisibility before they fade into the background.[2] This chapter focuses on three moments of controversy and hypervisibility that threatened the early days of the barcode, and I argue that these controversies are infrastructural echoes that resound again and again.

Consumer protests and the immediate backlash to the UPC

The Ad Hoc Committee solicited extensive feedback from industry stakeholders. They did not, however, give as much consideration to consumers. As an example, a confidential ten-page 1974 internal report that detailed the multi-year process only devoted a single paragraph to consumers.[3] The committee mostly assumed consumers wouldn't have strong feelings about barcodes, but the committee was very wrong. As Stephen Brown noted, the Ad Hoc Committee was "totally unprepared for the furor consumer groups were to raise."[4]

The furor began within months of the announcement of the UPC and well before most people had ever actually seen a barcode in a grocery store. The consumer-side of the UPC protests was spearheaded by Carol Tucker-Foreman, the leader of the Consumer Federation of America (CFA). Tucker-Foreman was a major figure in the early days of the barcode, and while counterfactuals are at best educated guesses, it's possible barcodes might have been adopted without much controversy if a less forceful individual led the CFA in the mid-1970s. As a member of the Ad Hoc Committee described Tucker-Foreman decades later, "she was a formidable adversary" whom the grocery industry was unprepared to fight.[5]

And quite a fight it was. From the announcement of the UPC in 1974 until she took a job as the US Assistant Secretary of Agriculture in 1977, Tucker-Foreman went on a national tour to fight against barcode adoption. She appeared on *The Phil Donahue Show* in 1974 to warn consumers about the black lines that might soon appear in their grocery stores, testified at a major US Senate hearing and various state legislatures, was quoted in countless newspaper articles, and participated in public debates with grocery industry representatives where they "verbally slugged it out." Tucker-Foreman believed that workers had unions to advocate for them, the grocery industry had lobbyists, but "the consumer is powerless."[6] Her point had merit, and industry insiders later recognized that they had not given consumers enough of a voice in the barcode planning process. To quote a 1979 industry report, consumers had "been mishandled and underestimated since the early stages of the Ad Hoc Committee."[7]

The consumer protests mostly focused on two issues. The first was straightforward and never gained as much traction:

consumer organizations worried the grocery industry would pass the cost of barcode systems onto customers and raise prices. The second issue is more complicated and became maybe the most significant threat the barcode ever faced: the removal of individual item pricing. Before barcodes, most grocery stores directly labeled items with prices. One of the grocery industry's main drivers in the push for barcodes was to remove individual item pricing and instead display prices on store shelves. If you've been to a grocery store this century, you know that shelf pricing won out. In the mid-1970s, however, the removal of individual item pricing was essentially a non-starter for the CFA and smaller consumer groups. As a 1975 article detailed, "consumer groups were gearing up for a fight" to ensure that individual item pricing remained the norm.[8]

Tucker-Foreman believed that replacing individual item pricing with shelf pricing would lead to a loss of financial transparency and consumer agency. As she argued in multiple interviews and in her US Senate testimony, shelf pricing would "totally remove the consumer privilege to shop comparatively."[9] She even linked the issue to one of the major concerns of the 1970s by arguing that removing individual item pricing would reduce price consciousness and increase inflation.[10] The grocery industry responded to the growing controversy by proposing a solution that—to put it kindly—did not go over well: they offered to provide grease pencils to consumers so they could write prices on items. That ill-fated idea further angered Tucker-Foreman, who responded that grease pencils were "typical of the 'public be damned' attitude the industry takes. It equates on the PR equivalency scale with 'let 'em eat cake.'"[11]

From a contemporary perspective, it might seem rather strange to devote multiple pages of a short book to a battle about whether price tags would appear directly on products or on store shelves. I'll admit that, even after reading through many pages of archival interviews and Congressional testimony about item pricing, the controversy still feels rather abstract to me as someone who grew up in a world with shelf pricing. Regardless, the fight over item pricing was one of the most important moments of juncture in the history of the barcode, and at points the rhetoric from both sides got heated. Consumer organizations distributed polemical pamphlets with titles like "A New Supermarket Ripoff," and editorials were published with titles like "You'll Never See Price Till You Get Your Total If Grocery Industry Changes Its Ways."[12,13] Once the grocery industry realized consumer groups were gaining traction in the court of public opinion, industry representatives started striking back through public statements and editorials of their own. For example, a high-ranking grocery official angrily accused consumer groups of engaging in "polemics" and "half-truths."[14] One of the snarkiest articles from this period claimed that the "CFA apparently speaks for a constituency that cannot read the price on the shelf."[15] Some coverage of the protests tended to be condescendingly dismissive to consumers who supposedly had "a general suspicion to anything connected to computers," and local protests and boycotts were occasionally dismissed as a "fight with the local luddites."[16]

For a while, it looked like Tucker-Foreman's message might be winning. In the mid-1970s, legislation mandating item pricing was passed by the House in Arkansas and individual bills were being considered by states such as New York and California. Michigan actually passed an item-pricing law that stayed on the books until 2011.[17] This unanticipated, widespread backlash raised significant concern in the grocery industry, with insiders worrying that the CFA-led protests would slow barcode adoption for years. Some reports went even further and worried that consumer backlash might halt barcode adoption altogether: "the feeling of industry observers is that supermarket executives have lost their enthusiasm for the [barcode] system."[18]

The easiest way for the grocery industry to quell consumer concerns would have been to acquiesce on item pricing. To many consumer advocates, that solution seemed so obvious that the refusal to do so felt like petty stubbornness. To quote one consumer advocate, "Prices on individual products would eliminate all resistance to UPCs. It's such a little thing; it's really hard to understand why the food industry wouldn't agree to it."[19] The problem was that item pricing was not "such a little thing." It was quite a big thing, and if the item pricing fight had gone differently it could have significantly altered the development of the last 50 years of identification infrastructure. While the grocery industry's official stance was that decisions on item pricing should be left up to individual stores, industry representatives strongly fought against legislation mandating item pricing. Removing item pricing was *that* important to the overall barcode project.

The core reason why boils down to money: installing barcode systems was a huge financial investment. Stores needed to install scanners and computerized checkouts and train employees; manufacturers had to pay to tag every item. Industry sources estimated it would cost individual stores around $200,000 to install barcode systems and would take multiple years to see a return on the investment.[20] Barcodes had to save money for the technology to make sense, and one of the ways they were expected to do so was by reducing the labor required to individually price tag items. After all, one of the major reasons the grocery industry began exploring barcode adoption in the first place was because retail labor costs had risen by 67% over the previous two decades.[21]

Consequently, there was little possibility of a permanent compromise between the grocery industry and the CFA. If consumer advocates had won and national laws had been passed that mandated individual item pricing, it's possible the grocery industry would have given up on barcodes because the systems would have few paths to financial viability. Or, as the president of Giant Foods testified in a 1976 hearing, "Your decision with reference to mandatory price marking will therefore have an important impact on the decision of the industry whether to proceed with our plans to implement the computer-assisted checkout system."[22] Taking that point a step further, if the industry's barcode push had failed, that failure might have had consequences that extended well beyond grocery stores. As discussed in chapter 2, two of the watershed moments in the barcode's history—the defense industry's LOGMARS system and the automotive industry's standardization of barcodes—were inspired by the success of the grocery industry.[23] While barcodes now may feel inevitable and uncontroversial, this period of consumer protest was a significant threat and a turning point for the technology. Barcodes survived physical protests outside grocery stores, major Senate hearings, public debates, and countless negative newspaper articles, but their survival felt far from inevitable in the mid-1970s.

Because of the protests, some grocery stores retained item pricing for a while, sometimes by choice and sometimes because of state laws. However, by the late 1970s, the protests had mostly faded from news coverage, possibly in part because Tucker-Foreman—the face of the fight against the UPC—resigned as the head of the CFA to become the US Assistant Secretary of Agriculture for food and consumer services. The protests also likely faded because once barcodes began appearing in stores consumers may have realized barcodes were not as significant a threat as had been feared. Regardless of the reason, no national legislation was ever passed, and grocery stores shifted to shelf pricing throughout the late 1970s and early 1980s. Barcodes had survived what was maybe the greatest threat they ever faced.

Labor, automation, and the perils of the barcode

The consumer protests surprised the grocery industry, but they were more prepared for protests from another group: the Retail Clerks International Union (RCIU). The Ad Hoc Committee knew labor unions opposed the UPC, and unlike with consumer groups, the committee had considered labor issues throughout the process. One of the primary areas of focus in the crucial 1971 report that decided barcodes were a viable option was the likelihood of reduced labor costs. After all, barcodes made little sense as an investment if they *didn't* impact labor.

When the UPC was finalized in 1974, the RCIU went on the offensive and argued that barcodes might eliminate up to 20% of all grocery store jobs, a warning that echoes many of the same labor concerns people face today about newer forms of automation. Reduced labor costs weren't the only reason to adopt barcodes—barcodes would also provide much more extensive data on product movement that would impact how inventory was managed—but labor issues were a significant reason the committee had been formed in the first place. Additionally, the labor impacts were about more than just cost. They were also about, well . . . being human. As discussed in chapter 2, James Ritty had invented the cash register to partially remove human agency from the checkout process. The barcode was a next step in that process that could further reduce the chance of human error, and some of the newspaper coverage pitted consumers against labor, somewhat perversely blaming retail clerks for bringing this situation upon themselves.

Despite occasional coverage that argued consumers would benefit from labor's struggles, the initial labor and consumer protests often felt so intertwined that some sources argued they were basically inseparable. Many of these arguments were blatantly sexist and focused on the fact that Carol Tucker-Foreman was married to the special counsel for the RCIU. A few newspapers used their relationship to imply, sometimes subtly and sometimes not so subtly, that the CFA's fight against barcodes was more about helping the RCIU than it was about protecting consumers.[24] In other words, newspapers repeatedly suggested that the actions of a powerful, prominent woman were being driven behind the scenes by her husband. As one prominent industry figure stated in an item-pricing hearing about consumer concerns, "The hidden agenda here—and let's be honest about it—has been the impact this system will have on organized labor."[25]

The repeated claim that consumer protests were secretly driven by labor weren't supported by much more than misogyny about Tucker-Foreman's personal life. Nevertheless, the grocery industry's attempt to dismiss consumer concerns as primarily driven by labor unions indicates how much more traction the consumer protests got compared to labor protests. As discussed in the previous section, consumer protests came genuinely close to significantly slowing barcode adoption; labor protests, on the other hand, never gained the same level of attention. Most primary coverage mentioned the possibility of lost jobs in a paragraph or two in longer articles about consumer concerns, and legislative hearings about the UPC tended to focus more on consumers than labor. Consequently, the labor protests fizzled without much fanfare by the late 1970s, in part because reports showed barcodes would not reduce labor forces by as much as unions had feared, and in part because consumer protests had lost traction. Placed in a broader context, labor union power had also begun to decay by the 1970s, which likely limited the RCIU's ability to mount a significant push against barcode adoption. However, while the RCIU protests did not stop barcode adoption, labor battles over barcodes were far from over.

The US postal battle of the early 1990s

Delivering mail has always been a complicated logistical endeavor. Even before houses and apartments had individual addresses, mail carriers developed complex delivery processes in the 19th century.[26] As populations grew, postal services developed more granular data points, such as Zip Codes and then Zip Codes +4. Considering that logistical complexity, it's not surprising that barcodes have become a core infrastructure for shipping and delivery. Two of the largest mail services—the US Postal Service (USPS) and the United Parcel Service (UPS)—even developed their own barcode symbols, and by 1990 Federal Express (FedEx) was the world's largest single user of barcode technology. Barcodes are now an essential part of how postage is managed all over the world. As a 2005 article about FedEx explained, "Key to all this tracking is the bar code. FedEx scans bar codes on domestic ground packages 10 to 12 times from the point of pickup to the end delivery. The number of scans is as high as 23 on international packages."[27]

In the early 1990s, barcodes were already important to how private mail carriers like FedEx and UPS managed logistics. The USPS, in contrast, was slower to adopt the technology and was facing a major crisis. The USPS's costs were outpacing federal funding, and the agency was struggling to compete with the efficiency of privatized mail delivery services. Faced with ballooning debt and a lack of federal support, the USPS decided to do what many organizations have done in similar situations: automate some of their labor. Just like with the grocery industry more than a decade earlier, the USPS turned to barcode systems as a solution. Also just like with the grocery industry, a labor union—in this case the American Postal Workers Union (APWU)—publicly fought against the threat of the barcode. To simplify the story a bit, the early 1990s battle between the APWU and the USPS had three main figures: Anthony M. Frank (the US Postmaster General), Moe Biller (the longtime head of the APWU), and barcode sorting systems.

The USPS began using barcodes in the 1980s on a relatively small scale. In the early 1990s, Frank proposed a massive expansion of mail barcoding and the use of automated sorting machines that would read barcodes and sort mail to increase efficiency. However, just like with the use of barcodes in grocery stores, efficiency wasn't the only—or arguably even the primary—driver of the proposed barcode investment. Rather, a major goal was to cut labor costs. As Frank stated in 1991 when discussing the new barcode system, "The job cutbacks will save the Postal Service $4.5 billion a year in salary and benefits by 1995," and "Automation is our passport to the future, and in many respects, the future is now."[28,29]

As the longtime head of the APWU, Biller launched a public offensive against Frank's barcode plans that received significant attention. On multiple occasions Biller called for Frank to resign because of his barcode plans and warned that the Postmaster General had no idea how many jobs the new system would cost. To make matters even worse for the APWU, Frank's plan contracted out the labor required to barcode mail, further angering the union. According to Biller, the plan to use barcodes to automate mail sorting was a direct attack on labor that would result in the loss of upwards of 100,000 jobs.[30]

The coverage of the fight between Biller and Frank—with barcodes stuck in the middle as the nonhuman actor—broke down along lines that feel like they could come from a 2020s article about a topic like driverless cars and automation. A few sources argued that the USPS was one of the largest sources of well-paid, middle-class jobs in the US and were sympathetic to the APWU. Most coverage, however, backed Frank's barcode plan and implied that Biller and the APWU were fighting against progress. As the title of one editorial declared, "Postal Automation Cannot Be Held Back."[31] In the 1970s, barcodes were a struggling curiosity; by the early 1990s, they were being treated as an inevitability.

Biller argued that he was not against automation and that "we know automation is here to stay, but there doesn't have to be a loss of jobs."[32] The issue was that, similarly to item pricing in the 1970s, there wasn't much room for compromise. The proposed barcode system was too expensive—estimates predicted it would cost around $4 billion in capital costs—to implement if it wasn't going to cut labor costs. And just like with the RCIU more than a decade earlier, the APWU did not win its fight against barcode systems. The USPS implemented Frank's barcode sorting system, and by 1991 the agency had already announced the elimination of tens of thousands of jobs, with many more jobs eliminated in the following years.[33] In the battle between labor and the barcode, labor had lost once again.

Infrastructural echoes

These three examples are certainly not the only times barcodes were embroiled in controversy, but I chose them because they are an important part of the barcode's story.

The consumer protests in the 1970s represented a significant threat to the success of the barcode. Once technologies become taken-for-granted, there's often a tendency to act as if their success was almost inevitable. No technology—no matter how successful—is ever inevitable. Even the most widely adopted objects often face critical moments that could have changed their future if events had played out differently. Those moments of conflict and hypervisibility eventually become forgotten and erased by narratives of "inevitability" and technological determinism that shape so many popular understandings of technology.

The consumer protests of the 1970s were one of those moments, and a reminder that the invisibility of infrastructure is something that often must be earned, not assumed. Before barcodes could fade into the background, they had to survive this period of hypervisibility that could have significantly impacted the spread of the technology throughout the world in the 1980s.

The two labor protests discussed above were never as significant a threat to barcode adoption. Nevertheless, they show how difficult it can be for objects to become uncontroversial and ignored. Maybe most importantly, the labor protests are an important part of the barcode's story because they illustrate how the spread of the technology impacted many people's lives. Some workers affected by barcode adoption were fortunate enough to keep their jobs but had to learn new skills as their responsibilities changed. Many other workers weren't so lucky and became unemployed because barcode systems partially automated their labor. Decades later, many supermarkets moved to self-checkout systems that further hollowed out retail labor, a move that would have been impossible without near-total barcode adoption. The story of the barcode is partially a story of people whose labor was replaced and whose lives were negatively impacted by the implementation of those patterns of lines and spaces.

The labor part of the barcode's story also shows how little has changed in the previous decades. In industry after industry, companies have introduced new technologies to automate labor and reduce human labor costs. Barcodes are just one part of that much larger historical trend, a trend that will likely hasten in the coming years as technologies like driverless cars (if they ever exist) and AI-assisted writing possibly displace wide swaths of the labor market. Many of these technologies will likely automate labor at a scale that will make the barcode's impact look rather quaint, but the core concerns we face about automation in the 2020s are echoed in the fears about barcodes in the 1970s and 1990s. The widespread adoption of barcodes was a notable step in the history of automation, but it was a small step compared to what's coming.

5 PRESIDENT BUSH AND THE BARCODE

The protests of the 1970s contributed to slower-than-expected barcode adoption, and some observers predicted the barcode project might fail completely.[1] The barcode's fortunes began looking up in the early 1980s. By the end of 1981 more than 3,100 supermarkets had installed scanning systems.[2] In 1986 there were seven large US markets where more than sixty percent of all food sales were processed through barcodes, and sixty-four percent of all volume in large supermarkets came from stores with barcode systems.[3] The upward trend continued from there, and in 1989 more than half of all grocery store sales in the US relied on barcodes.[4] Outside the grocery industry, barcode adoption had expanded at an arguably even faster rate.[5] In just over a decade, barcodes had transformed from a near failure to one of the most rapidly adopted technologies in history.

Statistics about barcode adoption are an important illustration of success. However, statistics can only tell one part of the story of how quickly the barcode went from being a controversial curiosity to a widely accepted part of everyday life. Additionally, I don't particularly want to write an entire chapter about barcode adoption statistics, and I doubt many people would want to read that chapter. Rather than listing all the adoption statistics I could find, I instead want to turn in a different direction to illustrate the barcode's move towards learned invisibility (in the US, at least): the 1992 US presidential election.

The 1992 US presidential election was filled with twists and turns. At one point, third-party candidate Ross Perot seemed like the frontrunner, but he dropped out of the race for bizarre reasons only to restart his campaign one month before the election. Perot ended up getting the highest share of the popular vote of any third-party presidential candidate since Teddy Roosevelt in 1912. Bill Clinton weathered multiple scandals and positioned himself as a man of the people on his way to a solid victory in November. The incumbent President George H.W. Bush went from a historically high eighty-nine percent approval rating in the Spring of 1991 to losing the election fourteen months later. The election did not lack drama, and rather surprisingly, the barcode became a key storyline in a presidential race filled with sex scandals, accusations of draft dodging, and recession fears.

President Bush's fall in 1992 was almost unprecedented in US presidential history. In less than 18 months, he went from one of the highest approval ratings of all time to losing in an electoral landslide. Commentators typically pointed to two related explanations for Bush's precipitous decline: a slumping economy and the perception that he was out of touch.[6] Whereas Clinton successfully spun his famous "I feel your pain" messaging, Bush struggled to overcome the narrative that he was an elite who did not understand "regular" Americans. An incident that helped cement that narrative centered on, of all things, a barcode.

In February 1992, President Bush visited a National Grocers Association convention and was shown a barcode and a barcode scanner. Then—according to a front-page article in the *New York Times*—the following incident occurred:

> Today, for instance, he [President Bush] emerged from 11 years in Washington's choicest executive mansions to confront the modern supermarket . . .
>
> He grabbed a quart of milk, a light bulb and a bag of candy and ran them over an electronic scanner. The look of wonder flickered across his face again as he saw the item and price registered on the cash register screen.
>
> "This is for checking out?" asked Mr. Bush. "I just took a tour through the exhibits here," he told the grocers later. "Amazed by some of the technology."[7]

While that short passage may seem rather innocuous, it had a significant impact on Bush's presidential run.

Throughout the 1992 campaign, the media and opposing politicians used the barcode story as a symbol of Bush's lack of knowledge about "normal" American life. Within a few days of that fateful convention, editorials lambasting Bush for not knowing how to shop in the modern supermarket began popping up everywhere. Less than a week later a *Washington Post* article joked that "If all the other bozos running for the presidency are as ignorant about American life as George Algernon Fortesque Leffingwell Bush proved himself to be last week, then this much is certain: The country really is going to hell, not in a handbasket but in a shopping cart." Hillary Clinton brought up the barcode incident to contrast Bush to her husband, and late-night comedy shows used the story of Bush and the barcode to make joke after joke about how the President was so out of touch that he didn't even know how to buy his own groceries. That one interaction with a barcode dogged Bush for the rest of his reelection campaign, and even more surprisingly, the rest of his life.

After Bush lost the 1992 election, political analysts James Carville and Paul Begala's election post-mortem highlighted the barcode incident as a prime example of Bush's failure to connect with the American public.[8] The barcode story was then repeated again and again in the following decades. For example, a 2014 *CNN* article cited Bush's barcode interaction as the top example of recent presidential gaffes.[9] The barcode story even made an appearance in the former president's *New York Times* obituary when he died in 2018: "His critics saw him as out of touch with ordinary Americans, pointing to what they portrayed as his amazed reaction during a demonstration of a supermarket scanner when he visited a grocers' convention while president."[10] Even in death, Bush could not escape that barcode.

But here's the problem . . . the story about Bush and the barcode was mostly nonsense.

What actually happened with President Bush and the barcode

The *New York Times* journalist who wrote the front-page story about Bush and the barcode—Andrew Rosenthal—had not attended the convention where the incident occurred. In fact, only one national journalist had attended the grocer's convention, likely because it was a grocer's convention. That journalist filed a two-paragraph pool report about the event, and Rosenthal's entire story was based off a short sentence in the report that simply said Bush had a look of "wonder" when he was shown a barcode and a scanner. Rosenthal took that one mention and wrote an entire front-page story with vivid details about Bush's amazement at simple barcode technology, and his story was then picked up by paper after paper and became fodder for Democratic operatives.

Rosenthal's portrayal of the event left out crucial details. Bush did attend the grocer's convention, and he did express amazement at the barcode technology he was shown. The problem was that the barcode system Bush said he was "amazed" by wasn't the typical barcode system that by 1992 had become mundane to so many Americans. Rather, Bush was reacting to a state-of-the-art scanner that could read crumpled up barcodes with precision. He was right to be amazed! That small detail is a crucial one, and it was mostly ignored during the 1992 presidential race.

Bush's political team quickly realized the emerging barcode story was going to be a problem. His press secretary angrily claimed that the President had "seen those [barcode scanners] many times. This a story that is totally media manufactured and maintained."[11] The *Associated Press* ran a story debunking the *New York Times*' coverage that quoted the man who showed Bush the scanner: "The whole thing is ludicrous. What he was amazed about was the ability of the scanner to take that torn label and reassemble it."[12] Other outlets reviewed the tape of the incident and called the whole thing overblown, stating that Bush looked impressed but certainly had no look of wonder "flickering across his face."[13] But none of those corrections mattered. No matter how many people tried to debunk the original story—there's even a 2001 *Snopes* fact check about it—the narrative was established, and the damage was done.

Barcodes as symbol for the "normal" America

The misrepresentation of President Bush's barcode moment is tame compared to conspiracies about the Clintons' supposed kill lists or Barack Obama's imaginary Kenyan birthplace. Nonetheless, the story played a significant role in the 1992 election because of the unique intersection of the public's impression of President Bush and the US public's relationship to the barcode that had developed by 1992. A random interaction with a scanner and a crumpled barcode was not *the* reason Bush lost the election. On its own, Bush's opponents almost certainly could not have used that one moment to paint the President as out of touch with the American public. Rather, the barcode story was persuasive because it built on a narrative about Bush that already existed for various reasons: Bush grew up in a rich New England family, he had a fairly aloof personality, and he had been a major political figure in Washington, DC for decades. The barcode story drew from that existing perception of Bush as out of touch, which became even more damaging as Americans struggled with an economy teetering on the edge of a recession in 1992. One *Washington Post* article even acknowledged that the barcode story might not be true but argued it didn't matter because it *felt* true: "Whatever Bush's true reaction to the scanner was that day, we all 'know' that this man has not bought a bag of groceries in a supermarket in at least 12 years of cloistered White House existence."[14]

That one moment also transformed into something bigger than Bush himself and became a symbol for the problem with "political elites" more broadly. A *New York Times* article titled "The Two Nations" used the barcode incident as a jumping off point to criticize "elites" for everything from failing to pass comprehensive healthcare reform to education reform. As the article argued, "the episode of the President and the unfamiliar supermarket suggests a broader point, a much more serious one."[15] And that's just one example of many in the leadup to the 1992 election. The President's brief encounter with a barcode and a scanner morphed into a powerful symbol for the elite political class's disconnection from "normal" American life.

The barcode story, however, wasn't resonant solely because of the public's perception of President Bush or political elites. The story was so resonant because of how thoroughly the barcode had become entwined in the fabric of everyday life for so many Americans. In the 1970s, groups were protesting barcodes and experts in the grocery industry feared the barcode would fail; by 1992, the barcode was ordinary and ubiquitous enough that it momentarily became a defining symbol of the division between political elites and "normal" Americans. Or, as Hillary Clinton put it in a 1992 interview, "It is a new time for the presidency to recognize the reality of people's lives. And it's not just about me. It's about not knowing there are scanners in grocery stores."[16]

It would be fairly straightforward to point to adoption statistics to mark the point when the barcode became an accepted, mostly unremarkable part of everyday life. However, while those statistics are obviously important, I argue that President Bush's fateful run-in with a barcode in 1992 was a moment that helped crystallize the barcode as a taken-for-granted part of people's lives. A technology shrouded in controversy a little more than a decade earlier had become so ordinary by the early 1990s that (supposed) unfamiliarity with it became a black mark that followed a US President for the rest of his life. The barcode had transformed from the "mysterious black lines" appearing at grocery stores to a symbol of "normal" American life, a symbol so potent that it played a role in bringing down one of the most powerful people in the world.

The often-misleading coverage of that brief barcode incident must have annoyed the former President to no end, and Bush "blamed the news media for the perception that he was out of touch with the average American."[17] But Bush managed to maintain at least some sense of humor about the whole thing. In the summer of 1992, after months of negative coverage and countless jokes about how amazed he was by barcodes, Bush presented the National Medal of Technology to Joseph Woodland for the role he played in inventing the barcode. At the presentation, Bush looked at Woodland and joked, "You've seen firsthand how impressed I am about how barcoding works. Amazing."[18]

6 BARCODES AND THE BIBLE

And he [the Beast] causeth all, both small and great, rich and poor, free and bond, to receive a mark in their right hand, or in their foreheads:

And that no man might buy or sell, save he that had the mark, or the name of the beast, or the number of his name.[1]

When I first started researching barcodes, I didn't think I'd eventually begin a book chapter with a Bible verse. Yet the more deeply I immersed myself in the history of the barcode, the clearer it became that the short passage above is an important part of the barcode's story. The passage is found about halfway through the final book of the New Testament—The Book of Revelation—and describes what is often referred to as "The Mark of The Beast." Revelation is a rather unique biblical text that is in part an apocalyptic prophecy of a Beast rising from the sea and waging a war against God.[2] The apocalyptic imagery of Revelation— which includes the Seven Seals, the Whore of Babylon, and the Four Horsemen of the Apocalypse—has made an indelible impact on Christianity and pop culture more generally. Few of the images have had as enduring an impact as the Mark of the Beast, a piece of prophecy that, almost two thousand years after Revelation was written, was interpreted in a way that placed the barcode at the center of a vast global conspiracy.

The apocalyptic prophecy detailed in Revelation focuses on a beast that will "rise up out of the sea, having seven heads and ten horns, and upon his horns ten crowns, and upon his heads the name of blasphemy."[3] The beast, which is often referred to as the Antichrist even though the term does not appear in Revelation, will be powered by Satan and align with a "second beast" that represents the false prophet. Together, the Beast and the false prophet will gather an army of followers to battle with God, and their followers will be identified by the "Mark" and the "number of his name" (often interpreted as 666).[4] The followers who take the Mark will eventually be left behind to suffer as the true believers ascend to heaven. If the Christian apocalypse ever happens, you don't want to be someone who took the Mark.

The passage describing the Mark is one of the most debated pieces of biblical prophecy, in part because so much is left up to interpretation. Within a year of the creation of the UPC, an interpretation arose in some evangelical Christian communities that the barcode *is* the Mark foretold in Revelation. As a 1975 article in the publication *Gospel Call* cautioned, the Mark of the Beast "COULD look like the strange markings on packages at supermarkets" and warned that these "strange markings" will eventually be "'laser tattooed' on the forehead or the back of the hand, which will be read by infrared scanners installed at the checkout counters."[5] The evangelical narrative linking barcodes to the end times only grew from there, and this chapter examines how the humble barcode became the target of an enduring religious conspiracy theory about the end of the world.

Reading 666 between the lines

Even as barcode adoption struggled in the 1970s, evangelical warnings continued to get louder. A 1978 section in the *Lexington Leader*, for example, advertised a "Prophecy Now!" event that asked "Are we living in the end times?" and then followed with "What is the strange code (UPC) on products we now buy?"[6] One rather combative letter to the editor in a Cedar Rapids, Iowa newspaper criticized Christian leaders for focusing their attention on the wrong places: "While pastors, lay people, and concerned people picket against the evils of pornography, a greater evil is spreading across our land . . . Behold, Cedar Rapids, you are becoming the birthplace of the Mark of the Beast: the UPC system."[7] You read that right: according to some evangelicals, the UPC barcode was worse than pornography.

While various articles and sermons claimed the barcode might be the Mark of the Beast, maybe the most influential person to popularize the idea was the evangelical author Mary Stewart Relfe. Her book *The New Money System* argued that the UPC barcode was a harbinger of the end times and warned that "the world's greatest conspiracy is being quietly conducted in the most sacred halls of secular secrecy."[8] According to Relfe, the biblical passage, "And that no man might buy or sell, save he that had the mark," meant that the move to a cashless society indicated the beginning of the end times foretold in Revelation. Relfe argued that the UPC barcode *was* the Mark and "would be the basic juggernaut of a cashless society."[9] She also believed that using barcodes to identify products was merely a first step; soon barcodes would be used to track humans through barcoded identification cards and barcodes tattooed onto people's bodies (most likely on their hand or forehead). Those who refused the Mark would be kept out of this "new money system" and would be unable to buy anything.[10]

Relfe's most enduring legacy was a detail of her conspiracy that still haunts the barcode to this day, a detail she attributed to a moment of divine revelation: "Like a flash of lightning I SAW IT. The Code was BROKEN. It was as easy to see as the sun on a clear day."[11] Her divine revelation was that the symbol was designed so that every single UPC barcode contained the Number of the Beast: 666. She may not have been the first to make that argument, but her claim remains influential more than four decades later. To this day, you can find various evangelical websites that argue that 666 is embedded in every single UPC and EAN barcode scanned at a supermarket. Her claim is a prime example of how a basic misunderstanding of an object can shape people's views in intractable ways.

To explain Relfe's divine inspiration, I want to return to the image of the UPC barcode found in chapter 3. As a brief reminder, the IBM symbol contains fifteen pairs of lines that contain twelve digits. The pairs of lines on the left, center, and right of the barcode do not contain actionable data; they are guard bars that provide reference points for scanners. However, when Relfe looked at the UPC, she saw a vast conspiracy concealed in those three pairs of guard bars found on billions of barcodes. According to her book, each of those guard bars were the line patterning for the number "6," so every single UPC barcode had a 666 embedded in its lines. The Number of the Beast was hidden in plain sight.

Relfe's reading of the UPC barcode was obviously incorrect; the members of the Ad Hoc Committee were not leaders of a global conspiracy designed to trick people into taking the Mark of the Beast (though it is somewhat amusing to imagine a group of grocery executives at the center of an apocalyptic conspiracy). Nonetheless, her book helped popularize an idea that became prominent on the fringes of evangelical culture and made the barcode the target of religious protests for decades. While these worries may have been based on a misreading of a few pairs of lines, that does not mean that they were any less genuine. A rather striking display of these fears was captured by the artist Eleanor Dickinson. Dickinson was a famous chronicler of Appalachian Revivalism in the 1980s who documented evangelicals' intense reaction to the barcode. She created what she called her "Mark of the Beast series" that consisted of drawings exhibited at museums across the United States. As one review of the series stated, "The images of her show are people facing their own endings, whether it be divorce or death, and the black bars of the UPC become rhythmic striations, part of her work."[12] One piece in particular captures evangelical fears about the barcode rather beautifully: the drawing depicts an elderly man holding a skull as a symbol of his imminent death, with a UPC barcode looming prominently in the background as a sign of the end of days.[13]

The legacy of the barcode and the Mark of the Beast

Evangelical fears were never a serious threat to the spread of the barcode, though some evangelical communities did protest outside grocery stores that used barcodes. Barcodes also weren't the only object that had been identified as the potential Mark—other examples include everything from social security numbers to driver's licenses—but they have been the most enduring.[14] More than forty years after these fears were first publicized, the link between the barcode and the Mark of the Beast still exists in some forms today.

Evangelical fears about the Mark of the Beast have shifted some over the years. In some cases, the barcode was replaced in evangelical narratives by Radio Frequency Identification (RFID) tags, a newer, more powerful identification technology. The shift from barcodes to RFID as the possible Mark began in the 1990s and gained steam throughout the 2000s, with multiple books arguing that the barcode warnings were misinterpretations of Revelation's prophecy, and RFID tags were the *actual* Mark foretold in Revelation.[15] Yet even many of these warnings about RFID did not abandon the barcode narrative completely. While books like *Beast Tech* and *New World Order* acknowledged that the barcode was not likely the "true" Mark, they still argued that barcodes had been invented to pave the way for acceptance of the actual Mark of the Beast.[16] To quote the book *Beast Tech*, barcodes were created to "condition mankind for nearly everything in the world—both animate and inanimate—being marked, tagged, coded, numbered, implanted, and identified."[17]

But not everyone moved away from the barcode as the Mark of the Beast. The enduring legacy of the narrative became particularly hard to ignore when Joseph Woodland— the "father" of the barcode—died in 2012 at 91 years old. As a *Wired* article titled "Why the Bar Code Will Always Be the Mark of the Beast" documented, some evangelical websites celebrated Woodland's death, and the comment sections in articles about Woodland's passing were flooded with accusations that he had Satanic connections.[18] Even today, one can easily find niche evangelical websites that argue the barcode *is* the Mark, and most of these sites still rely on Relfe's misreading of guard bars as their evidence. At almost fifty years old, the barcode is still entwined in fears of a global conspiracy based on an almost two-thousand-year-old biblical prophecy. For most people, barcodes are a technology so ubiquitous that they barely warrant a second thought; for others, those same barcodes can be a possible sign of the end of the world.

7 THE CULTURAL IMAGINARY OF THE BARCODE

Barcodes are a bit of a paradox. They are ignored yet iconic. They are a prime example of the learned invisibility of infrastructure yet also a prominent symbol of cultural critique in everything from popular science fiction to tattoos. As Roman Mars explained on his podcast *99% Invisible*, "for some people, the barcode has come to represent everything they hate about capitalism and consumerism . . . When I was a punk kid if a band's album had a barcode on it, we knew they were complete sell outs."[1] I was never quite *that* punk when I was a kid, but to return to the story that began book, I thought it was a super deep cultural statement when my high-school friend got a barcode tattoo on the back of her neck. It wasn't until I started researching barcodes two decades later that it occurred to me how bizarre it was that an object most closely associated with grocery stores became such a potent symbol that people would have it tattooed on their bodies.

This chapter explores how barcodes became an often-dystopian symbol of capitalism, conformity, and control by first examining science fiction and then turning to examples from the art world that used barcode iconography as cultural critique. However, the barcode's transformation into a shorthand image for the ills of capitalism is only one part of the story. As I also detail, plenty of people have adapted barcode imagery out of appreciation rather than criticism. Designers have playfully adapted barcodes on packaging, architects and artists have used barcodes as a design aesthetic, large online communities celebrate barcode designs, and some couples even get matching barcode tattoos to celebrate their anniversary. The barcode's place in the broader cultural imaginary is partially a story about critiques of consumption and conformity, but it's also a story of appreciation and celebration. Barcodes contain more than identification data; there's a whole lot of deeper cultural meaning embedded in those patterns of lines and spaces.

A symbol of dystopia

Barcodes began appearing in science fiction movies even before some screenwriters knew what they were called. Maybe the first prominent example was James Cameron's 1984 film *The Terminator*. The movie begins in a dystopian future where machines have enslaved most of the human population, and the few remaining free humans have formed a militant resistance led by a man named John Connor. The machines decide the best way to stop the human resistance is to send a machine (the Terminator) back in time to 1984 to murder John Connor's mother before he was born. The humans respond by sending a man named Reese to 1984 to protect John's mother, Sarah. Reese eventually finds her and must convince her that he's from the future in one of the movie's pivotal scenes. He does so by rolling up his sleeve and showing Sarah a barcode tattooed on his arm. He tells her the symbol was used in the machine's prison camps and was "burned in by laser scan. Some of us were kept alive . . . to work." As an illustration of how quickly barcodes started being used as a larger cultural symbol, James Cameron possibly didn't even know the word for the barcode or the UPC when he wrote the screenplay for *The Terminator*. As Cameron's script describes the scene, "Reese reveals a ten-digit number etched on the skin of his forearm. Beneath the numbers is a pattern of lines like the automatic-pricing marks on product packages."[2]

The Terminator was the first movie to feature a barcode tattoo I could find (though there might have been earlier films), and the movie likely influenced many other examples of dystopian science fiction that used barcode imagery. In 1992's *Alien 3*, the prisoners at a futuristic penal colony have barcodes tattooed on the backs of their heads. When one prisoner tells the main character Ripley that he isn't a prisoner, she sarcastically responds with "Then what about the barcode on the back of your head?" Similarly, Bruce

Willis' character in the 1995 movie *Twelve Monkeys* has a barcode tattoo on his neck to symbolize his loss of autonomy as a prisoner in a dystopian future. And those are just a few examples of the trope. Throughout 80s and 90s science fiction, barcodes were often used to symbolize dystopian forms of surveillance and control.[3]

The barcode as a symbol of control was only one way the object was deployed in science fiction. Barcodes also became a symbol for a different type of dehumanization: mass production and commodification. In the 2000s cult classic television show *Dark Angel*, a group of genetically modified humans have barcode tattoos on the back of their necks to show they are "owned" by the secret military organization that created them. The show's promotional materials prominently displayed barcoded bodies, implying that the protagonists were seen as products by the organization that created them.

The tattoos in *Dark Angel* use similar symbolism as another of the most iconic uses of barcode tattoos in science fiction: the wildly successful *Hitman* video game series that was adapted into two movies. The main character in *Hitman* is Agent 47, a bioengineered clone with a prominent barcode tattoo on the back of his shaved head. Just like in *Dark Angel*, the tattoo represents both mass production and the commodification of the body, with an implicit warning that the property rights of capitalism could someday spread to human bodies themselves. And while neither *Dark Angel* nor *Hitman's* use of barcode imagery is exactly subtle, the film *Repo Men* (2010) makes the symbolic link between barcodes and bodily commodification crystal clear. The movie depicts a future in which a corporation has invented artificial organs and sells them to patients at exorbitant interest rates. Once the patients can't pay their bill, the Repo Men show up, cut the patients open, and repossess the organs. Each organ has a barcode that the Repo Men have to scan as soon as it's removed from the body. The movie climaxes with a scene where the main character cuts himself open and shoves a barcode scanner inside his body to scan the barcode on his heart. It's not exactly subtle.

A different type of movie that features barcode tattoos is Mike Judge's *Idiocracy* (2006). Like the examples mentioned above, *Idiocracy* takes place in a dystopian future, but unlike those examples, *Idiocracy* is a comedy. The plot focuses on a man who goes into hibernation in 2005 and wakes up in 2505 in a world where people have become far less intelligent because of mass commercialism. In that future, everyone has a barcode tattooed on their hand, which the script specifically refers to as a "UPC." The barcode simultaneously symbolizes the conformity of a society that has stopped thinking critically while also working as shorthand for mass commercialism taken to comic heights. The main character is marked as different because he does not have a barcode tattoo, which both restricts his ability to move freely and signifies that he is a free thinker in contrast to the conformity of everyone around him.

By no means is this section a comprehensive compilation of science fiction that features barcode tattoos. There are more examples than I could hope to track down (or would ever want to watch), and barcodes still occasionally pop up in science fiction despite the widespread availability of more advanced tracking and identification technologies (e.g., the series of young adult novels called the *Barcode Tattoo Trilogy*).[4] More recently, barcode tattoos have mostly been usurped in science fiction imaginaries by microchip implants, with at least ten movies produced post-2010 featuring microchip implants to symbolize the types of conformity and control previously linked to barcodes. Nonetheless, barcodes were a prominent symbol in popular science fiction for almost thirty years, and if an anthology show like *Black Mirror* had been made in the 1990s, I'm willing to bet we would have gotten a barcode episode.

Barcodes, art, and critique

Cultural critiques that drew from barcode iconography were not limited to science fiction. The art world also used barcodes to explore issues ranging from dehumanization to commodification. One of the examples most closely linked to the science fiction tattoos discussed above was Jewish artist Alfred Schechtner's depictions of the Holocaust. During the Holocaust, Nazis and their collaborators tattooed concentration camp prisoners with identification numbers to dehumanize them in their horrific system. In a controversial piece, Schechtner made the link between the barcode and

Holocaust tattoos explicit in a series of digitally morphed photographs titled "Barcode to Concentration Camp Morph." The series starts with a drawing of a barcode. The barcode drawing then morphs across six frames into a black-and-white drawing of WW2 concentration camp prisoners. As one art critic described the piece, "The larger message speaks of the bar-coding of human life, the transformation of beings into numbers."[5]

Schechtner's piece metaphorically linked barcoding to the dehumanization of concentration camp tattoos, but in some contemporary cases the link is sadly more than metaphorical. Barcode tattoos have been used in human trafficking to "brand" women, and in some cases the barcode tattoos can literally be scanned to show the victim's "price." The practice is common enough that a peer-reviewed nursing article used stories of nurses noticing barcode tattoos on human trafficking victims to provide guidelines to medical professionals on how to identify barcode tattoos used in human trafficking.[6]

The apparent prevalence of these cases inspired an artistic intervention by the University of Miami's School of Medicine to raise awareness about the practice. The campaign was heavily promoted during the 2020 Super Bowl weekend in Miami, Florida and involved distributing temporary barcode tattoos to increase the visibility of human trafficking victims. The campaign chose the barcode because, according to a member of the project, "Barcodes are one of the major types of branding marks by traffickers. Many of these barcode tattoos will scan with a smartphone, placing a monetary value to that individual." Rather than using a typical barcode, the temporary tattoos depicted a "shattered barcode" to symbolize the possibility of breaking free from the dehumanization of human trafficking.[7]

Not all artistic adaptations of barcodes used the technology to explore issues of dehumanization. Other artists incorporated barcodes into their work to critique consumerism. For example, artist Mark Kelner created an exhibit he called *Barcodes/The Container* in response to the 2017 sale of a Leonardo Da Vinci painting for $450,000,000. The exhibit featured pieces that transformed the figures in famous works from artists like Da Vinci, Gaugin, and Modigliani into barcode lines set against white backgrounds. Kelner's work is a direct critique of the consumerism of the art world, and he chose barcodes as his medium to criticize the "uneasy marriage and paradox between art, money, fame, and power."[8] The transformation of famous pieces of art into barcodes "incongruously hits home this emblematic idea of how art is objectified, commodified, who owns it and why, and, above all, our relationship with these images and their inevitable appropriation and distortion."[9]

While Kelner's pieces used barcodes as a symbol of consumerism in one exhibit, the artist Scott Blake— whom *The Independent* called "arguably the most well-known barcode artist"[10]—has made a career out of incorporating barcodes in his art. Blake has used barcodes in various ways, with one exhibit echoing Warhol's "Campbell's Soup Cans" series by displaying entire walls of UPC barcodes from popular foods. Many of Blake's other pieces incorporated barcode designs into detailed portraits. Unlike Kelner, who replaced the entire figures in famous painting with barcode lines, Blake's barcode portraits reproduce famous images while retaining their recognizable characteristics. From afar, the portraits look like photographs, but in a possible play on the dots of pointillism, upon closer inspection each portrait is made up of thousands of functional barcodes. For example, his portrait of Marilyn Monroe is comprised of 1,944 UPC barcodes taken from the 22 UPC barcodes found on the DVDs for the films in which Monroe appeared.[11] To quote University of Minnesota professor Steven McCarthy, "In an obvious commentary on the genetics of consumer culture, Blake turns photos of pop icons into deadpan black and white bar code portraits."[12]

Not all artists and designers, however, adapted barcode imagery as a form of cultural critique. As the next section explores, barcodes have also been incorporated into everything from fine art to architecture to tattoos for a very different reason: some people think they look cool.

The aesthetic pleasures of the barcode

The immediate recognizability of barcode iconography that has made them a potent symbol of critique has also made barcodes a popular design aesthetic. An example from the fine art world is the work of artist Bernard Solco, who created many huge displays of both linear and 2D barcodes shaded with vibrant colors. Solco's art explored the hidden beauty of barcode designs and was commissioned for display at various AIDC trade shows in the 1990s and 2000s.[13] Similarly, many graphic designers have adapted barcode symbols for their familiarity and aesthetic appeal. If you search for various social movements plus the word "barcode" on Amazon, you'll often find designs that adapt barcodes in colorful, playful ways. For example, Amazon features a long list of "Pride" stickers and temporary tattoos that use barcodes as a design element rather than, at least as far as I can tell, a symbol of critique.

Additionally, there are large online communities focused on the aesthetic appreciation of barcodes and the celebration of innovative tweaks to established symbols. Maybe the largest such community is the r/barcodeporn subreddit, which has more than 30,000 members.[14] R/barcodeporn is a space to share unique barcode designs (mostly of UPC-A and EAN-13 barcodes) and celebrate the malleability of the barcode as an object (see image 3 for a few examples). After all, while UPC and EAN barcodes may have become so recognizable because they're everywhere and almost always look the same, there are ways to play with barcode design while retaining their functionality. The examples shared in these online communities explore the aesthetic potential of the barcode, and r/barcodeporn is a space where people

IMAGE 3 Three barcode design adaptations. The barcode on the top left (used with the permission of reddit user SoftServeMeat) is used for a beer from Catawba Brewing Company. The barcode on the top right (used with the permission of reddit user CallMehZia) is used for a Smiltanis Drawing Pad. The barcode on the bottom (used with permission of reddit user EvilSuppressor) was found on a product at Sainsbury's.

celebrate innovative uses of a barcode symbol that has barely changed in fifty years.

Artists and designers adapting barcodes in their work might not be that surprising. After all, there are a whole lot of working artists and designers and a whole lot more barcodes moving through the world. More surprisingly, barcodes have also been used as aesthetic inspiration by major architectural firms that have created buildings to look like barcodes.

Barcode-inspired buildings can be found all over the world, including:

- **The Barcode Project (Oslo, Norway):** a major development of twelve narrow high-rise buildings that were built in 2016 to collectively resemble the design of different types of barcodes.

- **The Barcode Halls (Nanhui New City, China):** a series of giant buildings covered with the barcode's black lines and white spaces that were built as the aesthetic centerpiece of the newly planned city.

- **Shtrikh Kod (St. Petersburg, Russia):** a massive, rectangular red building with a façade modelled to look like a UPC barcode that even includes numbers on the façade to show what each line pairing represents.

These buildings, just like with barcode Pride stickers or playfully constructed UPCs, embrace and adapt the iconicity of the barcode for aesthetic appeal. And to bring this discussion full circle, I want to end where I began: barcode tattoos. As I covered earlier, science fiction directors and artists have used barcode tattoos to symbolize the dangers of capitalism and conformity, but barcode tattoos have a more malleable meaning than just critique. The reasons people get barcode tattoos vary widely and are often impossible to decipher without further context. Some people—like my high-school friend—tattoo barcodes on their body to, as one tattoo website puts it, "take a stance against the status quo of our modern corporate-driven society" and push back against "feeling like a cog in a machine."[15] On the other hand, plenty of people get barcode tattoos for sentimental reasons that have nothing to do with conformity or consumption. As that same tattoo website explains, some people get barcode tattoos that contain meaningful dates or the UPC number of a product that has some deeper personal resonance. Other people adapt barcode designs to depict everything from a city skyline to an individual's face. My favorite examples I found were "couple's barcode tattoos" where two people get matching barcode tattoos that contain the date of their anniversary.[16] As soon as this book is published, I'm going to get a barcode tattoo that contains the book's ISBN number to celebrate, and I know that people who see the tattoo will have no idea what it means unless they ask me. Such is the nature of barcode tattoos: they can represent everything from critiques of capitalism and conformity to a loved one's birthday or an appealing aesthetic element in a larger design.

The many meanings of the barcode

A significant reason for the barcode's symbolic power is the technology's ubiquity and immediate recognizability. Most people know what barcodes look like and what they do, so they can be used in myriad ways without requiring much explanation. Dystopian science fiction can put a barcode on screen to symbolize dehumanization, and the director can trust that audiences won't require extended exposition to understand what the barcode represents. Architects can design buildings based on barcode designs and assume people will likely understand the buildings' aesthetic influence.

The transformations of an identification technology into one of the most iconic symbols of capitalism and a source of aesthetic appreciation in online fan communities are some of the more surprising parts of the barcode's story. Barcodes occupy an almost paradoxical position in the cultural imaginary that highlights the complex in/visibility dynamics of infrastructural objects. They are simultaneously a pervasive, mostly ignored object people barely pay attention to *and* an immediately recognizable icon of capitalism and conformity *and* a form of artistic expression. The fact that patterns of lines and spaces can mean so many things to so many people is a testament to the barcode's impact not just as a data infrastructure, but as an icon that carries far more cultural weight than its initial proponents could have ever imagined.

8 THE LONG AND WINDING ROAD OF THE QR CODE

When I tell people that I've been writing a book about barcodes, I often get asked some variation of, "But aren't QR Codes going to replace barcodes soon?" QR Codes seemed to rise from the ashes like a Phoenix in the early days of the Covid-19 pandemic. Suddenly they were replacing restaurant menus, appearing on countless printed materials, and even popping up in Super Bowl commercials about cryptocurrencies. To someone unfamiliar with the history of QR Codes, it made a certain sense to assume they were a cool new thing that might soon replace the fifty-year-old barcodes people grew up scanning.

There are multiple reasons QR Codes can't replace barcodes, the most glaring of which is that QR Codes *are* barcodes. They're a 2D barcode technology, and they're not the only 2D barcodes in wide use today. Additionally, QR Codes aren't new. They were first invented in 1994 and were hyped in the Western world in the mid-2000s until they failed so spectacularly that they became a cautionary tale about new technologies no one wanted. Even as QR Codes mostly disappeared in much of the West in the early 2010s, they were widely adopted elsewhere. In China in particular, QR Codes have been popular for years, and more than 90% of all Chinese mobile payments occur through apps that use QR Codes.[1] QR Codes are not an upstart newcomer here to replace established barcode symbols. They are themselves an established barcode symbol.

Another reason QR Codes haven't replaced older forms of barcodes—and likely won't anytime soon—is possibly the most interesting: bigger isn't always better, and more data isn't always better data. While QR Codes (and other 2D barcodes) are more powerful than linear barcodes, the simplicity of a standard like the UPC or the EAN can be a feature rather than a bug in many contexts. In other contexts, the increased data capacity of QR Codes has made novel uses of barcode technology possible, and many of those contexts focus on interactions with smartphones rather than scanners and supply chains. While most barcodes are bridges between objects and digital records, QR Codes have become a bridge between humans and the digital mediated through a smartphone screen.

The rest of this chapter explores the QR Code's role as a visible, and rather unique, example of barcode technology. I begin by first pointing out that QR Codes may be the most recognizable 2D barcode, but they are far from the only type widely used today. I then turn to the complicated history of QR Code adoption, a history of very public failure and eventual success. QR Codes are a barcode symbol that was left for dead and then seemingly rose from the grave in the Western world during a global pandemic.

The 2D revolution, delayed

When I spent a week doing research at Stony Brook University's George Goldberg archives, I devoted an entire day to combing through primary documents about 2D barcodes. I figured most of the documents would be focused on QR Codes because, to be honest, QR Codes were one of the only 2D barcodes I knew existed. My assumption seemed correct when I walked by at least three event flyers that featured QR Codes in the short hallway that led to the library's special collections room. When I sat down and started reading, I realized how wrong I was. QR Codes are the most visible example of 2D barcodes, but they arrived late to the party and are only one of the 2D barcodes adopted by various industries.

As discussed in chapter 3, linear barcodes have limited data capacity that is determined by patterns of lines and spaces. To add more data, you typically need to add more lines, which often means you need a bigger linear barcode. In part because of their data capacity limitations, many linear barcodes are "license plate" codes that transmit a number that links to a database entry that contains most of the information about the object. The barcodes themselves typically connect an object to more detailed information stored elsewhere.

Linear barcodes have been so successful in part because of that simplicity. However, the AIDC industry realized in the 1980s that some situations might require barcodes with much more data capacity. Consequently, companies began developing 2D barcodes that do not have to be read linearly and can contain a much denser amount of data in a smaller space. Unlike "license plate" codes that link to a database, 2D barcodes have the capacity to work as "annunciator codes" that contain significant data about an object. Whereas a UPC or EAN barcode might let someone access an entry where they could see an object's point of origin, a 2D barcode could contain information like point of origin and longer strings of records across the supply chain. 2D barcodes, in other words, can partially replace the more detailed database record and contain the relevant information in the symbol itself.

I want to briefly explain how 2D barcodes work to differentiate them from linear barcodes. There are two broad categories of 2D barcodes: stacked barcodes and matrix barcodes (see image 4). Stacked barcodes, which include symbols like PDF417 found on many driver's licenses, are a series of 1-dimensional barcodes miniaturized and layered on top of each other. The other category of 2D barcodes—matrix codes—is a more significant divergence from linear barcode symbols. Matrix codes, which include

IMAGE 4 Three types of 2D barcodes. The symbol on the left is a "stacked" PDF417 symbol, the middle symbol is a QR Code, and the symbol on the right is a Data Matrix barcode.

QR Codes and other widely used symbols like the Data Matrix, are typically square rather than rectangular and use a "checkerboard" pattern of black-and-white sections to encode data. While different matrix symbols feature various designs, they almost all include ways to detect the size of the code, correct for errors, and decode the position at which the code is being read. QR Codes and Data Matrix codes follow similar principles (see Image 4), but QR Codes rely on the distinctive squares for positioning whereas Data Matrix codes use the L-shaped solid black line to communicate positioning. Regardless of the minor differences, matrix codes can hold more data in a smaller space than linear and stacked barcodes.

The ability to contain significantly more data across two dimensions was appealing to various industries, and the first viable 2D barcode—Code 49—was developed in 1987.[2] Just two years later, the barcode industry newsletter *Scan* published an article about the "two-dimensional code sweepstakes" as companies rushed to develop 2D barcodes.[3]

Symbol Technologies, a mobile data capture firm, spent $50 million dollars developing the PDF417 barcode that was released in 1991.[4] UPS developed their own 2D barcode in 1992—the Maxicode—that is still used today. By the mid-1990s, the AIDC industry was in the middle of what the journal *ID Systems* called "2-D Codes' defining moment."[5] By then, there were more than ten 2D barcodes competing to become the standard in various industries.

QR Codes were a somewhat late entrant to the 2D sweepstakes. They were invented in 1994 by the Japanese company Denso Wave for use in the automotive industry, and they didn't make an immediate splash even after they were placed in the public domain. The industry publications I found didn't start mentioning QR Codes regularly until the late 1990s, and even then, the symbols mostly appeared in articles alongside other available 2D barcode options.[6] In other words, there were few indications in the early history of the QR Code to suggest that decades later they would become a core part of China's mobile transaction system and a major form of communication media in the Western world. And despite their eventual success, QR Codes are certainly not the only type of 2D barcode that shapes people's lives in often unnoticed ways. Next time you get a package or use a mobile boarding pass to get on a plane, pay attention to the 2D barcode. If it doesn't have the distinctive squares, it's not a QR Code; instead, the symbol is one the many other 2D barcodes that were jockeying for position when QR Codes were barely a blip on the AIDC radar.

While various 2D barcodes are in widespread use today, they never reached the levels of adoption some people in the AIDC industry expected in the 90s. As a 1995 industry report stated, "Clearly, the 2-D scanner market has failed to lift-off in spite of a great deal of publicity and promotion of the past four years."[7] The initial struggles surprised some experts who predicted 2D barcodes would replace linear barcodes because they were much more powerful.[8] 2D barcode adoption struggled for multiple reasons, some that could have been predicted and some that came as a surprise. A more predictable reason that limited 2D adoption was that most of the symbols couldn't be read by established scanners, so they needed to be decoded by either new laser technology or advanced camera technology combined with new software. They were an expensive investment, especially considering so many industries had already invested so many resources in linear barcode systems.

The technological challenges and costs were eventually mostly overcome, and now many smartphones can read 2D barcodes. However, 2D barcodes faced another issue that was less predictable: more data isn't always better data. Despite the seemingly common-sense observation that *of course* companies would want more data, that ended up not being the case in various industries where the "license plate" model persists to this day. What also likely helped less powerful linear barcodes survive—and what some 1990s observers understandably failed to predict—was the rise of the Internet. One of the major selling points of 2D codes was that they could contain most of the actionable information in the symbol itself, so organizations wouldn't have to rely on spotty telecom infrastructure to link to database records. That problem became less pronounced as the Internet became more widespread and wireless communication became faster and more efficient. Considering that history, it's somewhat ironic that decades later the most recognizable of all 2D barcodes—QR Codes—became a highly visible bridge between objects and the Internet.

The rise and fall and rise again of QR Codes

Most of the 2D barcodes discussed above extend barcode capabilities in areas they were already being used, such as logistics, identification, ticketing, and so on. In contrast, QR Code adoption shifted how people interact with barcode technology and has embedded barcodes in new domains. Most people don't recognize QR Codes because of anything to do with supply chains or inventory management; QR Codes have become so visible because they are the symbol that has enabled unique ways for people to connect with digital information.

Just like with older barcodes, QR Codes did not rise in isolation. The common uses of QR Codes are closely linked to the development of increasingly advanced mobile phone cameras and software processing power to decode the data contained in the symbols. After all, it's not a coincidence that QR Codes started getting hyped in the mid-2000s as more mobile phones had 3G connections and better cameras. As mobile communication scholar Leopoldina Fortunati argued, "with the mediation of the mobile phone, [QR Codes] can then act as a bridge between a static media (like a print newspaper) and a dynamic media."[9] Just as the original barcode symbol only became viable once lasers were invented, QR Codes—at least in the most visible ways they're often used now—only became mainstream once mobile phones became powerful enough to read them.

Technological adoption is rarely linear, and in few cases is that clearer than with the QR Code. As QR Codes began being hyped as a major new communication technology in the late 2000s, I distinctly remember when those mysterious symbols began popping up everywhere, even in one case on a syllabus when my professor was trying to be cool. QR Codes, however, are a classic example of "too much, too soon." In the mid-2000s, media industries, advertising firms, and small businesses poured money into QR Codes and academics published countless articles about their potential.[10] For a short period, it felt like they might be on the brink of widespread adoption. That period was short-lived, and QR Codes failed so thoroughly that they went from the "next big thing" to a literal joke.

By the early-2010s, articles declared that "the QR Code [was] dead" and used the QR Code as the poster child for overly-hyped technologies that no one wanted.[11] Comedians were doing stand-up bits about how silly the QR Code moment had been, and authors were even publishing books making fun of the marketing and media firms that had pushed QR Codes on a disinterested public. Maybe the most amusing example was the 2013 book *QR Codes Kill Kittens*, which humorously catalogued the many ridiculous ways companies had tried to use QR Codes to replace much easier ways to get information.[12] Part of the reason QR Codes failed was because their use was often based on a misunderstanding of how communication works. They were "rooted in a simple vision: the more communication there is, the better it is."[13] By the mid-2010s—in the West at least—it felt like QR Codes were already being lowered into their grave.

The many obituaries written in the 2010s were clearly premature, but even more than premature, they were myopically focused on the West. Even as QR Codes became a joke in much of the West, they were becoming omnipresent in China. China had developed its own 2D symbol called the Han Xin barcode, but it was the QR Code that became a crucial part of the Chinese media ecosystem. One of the main reasons the symbols became ubiquitous in China was because they were incorporated into the WeChat messaging and mobile payment service used by over a billion people.[14] By 2020, countless mobile payments in China used QR Codes, and the symbols could be found everywhere, even in some rather unexpected places. One 2017 image I found showed a member of a bridal party wearing a lanyard with a QR Code around her neck that guests could scan to give money as a wedding gift (that did not go over particularly well).[15] That's an extreme example, but it's emblematic of how QR Codes became an important part of the fabric of everyday Chinese life even as commentators in the West read their last rites.

So how did QR Codes reemerge in the West after becoming a cautionary tale of misplaced tech hype? One reason is that they became easier to scan. Until 2017, most smartphones required a separate application to scan QR Codes, and that barrier to entry was likely enough to make many people decide it wasn't worth it. In 2017, Apple integrated a QR Code reader function into the iPhone's camera app, and many Android phones did so not long after. People could then skip the extra step of opening a separate app and could scan QR Codes directly.

Including QR Code readers in default camera apps played a role in the QR Code's resurgence, but technological changes can only explain so much. After all, it's not as if QR Codes saw a huge explosion of usage between 2017 and 2019; by 2017, many people had already given up on the technology, and not even iPhone integration could bring them back. But then the unexpected happened when Covid-19 started spreading in early 2020. The rise of QR Codes in the West is closely linked to the pandemic in part because of a rather curious reason: a misunderstanding of how the virus spread that—well after the theory had been debunked—continued to shape public health discourse. Not only was QR Code adoption linked to a global pandemic, it was spurred in part by an incorrect theory about Covid-19 that seemingly would not go away.

In the early days of the pandemic, scientists theorized that Covid-19 spread primarily through touch. Much of the early public health messaging focused on hand washing to slow the spread, and people were instructed not to touch surfaces. I vividly remember trying to buy hand sanitizer in March 2020 and finding that it was sold out everywhere I went. QR Codes appeared all over the place in those early days of our new, supposedly "touchless" society. Many restaurants replaced paper menus that might transmit the virus with QR Codes people could scan to access menus on their phones. Companies switched from marketing through print materials to having people scan QR Codes because even touching a piece of paper was supposedly risky. These data-rich symbols suddenly had a well-defined purpose in a world where touch was supposedly dangerous. Marketing research found that the percentage of Americans who had scanned QR Codes jumped by 25% from 2019 to 2020.[16] A 25% year-to-year increase would be impressive for any technology, but it's especially impressive for a technology that was more than twenty-five years old.

By the late summer of 2020, the scientific consensus had determined that Covid-19 didn't spread much through touch, but by that point it barely mattered. People were getting used to scanning QR Codes and companies came up with impactful ways to use them. In addition, it's hard to change people's minds after initial messaging, so the "touchless" messaging held weight long after the scientific consensus shifted. Businesses and schools continued to advertise their "deep cleaning" procedures to stop surface spread throughout 2021, cities closed down outdoor playgrounds throughout 2021, and even as late as May 2022 I went to a conference with a "no handshaking" policy designed to stop the spread of the virus, scientific consensus be damned. The fears of touch were seemingly here to stay, and QR Codes were one of the huge beneficiaries.

QR Codes also became a prominent part of the pandemic because multiple countries used the symbols to do everything from verify vaccine status to record who entered locations for contact tracing purposes. Initially, some countries focused on more technologically complex systems like Bluetooth tracking to monitor people's movement and close contacts. However, most of these systems failed in part because of privacy concerns about surveillance. QR Codes became a compromise in countries like Australia that shelved earlier plans and turned to less invasive systems to record movement and close contacts. These national systems likely played a role in normalizing scanning QR Codes as part of daily life.

With continuing worries about touch and the normalization of QR Codes, people's willingness to scan the symbols has only continued to increase. As multiple publications argued, 2021 was the "Year of the QR Code."[17] A technology that, at least in the West, had been an overhyped failure had finally found its place in the media ecosystem.

In just the single day before I first drafted this paragraph, I encountered QR Codes on the rapid antigen tests in my pantry, the counter of the brewery by my house, the Venmo app I use to pay our dog sitter, the animal shelter flyer in my mailbox, and even the business card of my exterminator. That's not a bad second act for an object that was seen as a joke a decade ago.

QR Codes and second acts

The history of technology is filled with objects that were hyped, became disappointments, and then were eventually adopted. That history is also filled with objects designed for one purpose that ended up being used in unexpected ways. Even within that historical context, the QR Code stands out. They are an almost 30-year-old technology that were such a disappointment that by the early 2010s people were writing entire books making fun of them. Additionally, when they were invented in 1994 to track parts in the Japanese automotive industry, few people could have imagined how they'd be used today. The World Wide Web was only a few years old and mobile phones were still in their infancy. The gap between what QR Codes were invented for and what they have become is massive.

At almost 30 years old, QR Codes finally feel established in the West, and their resurgence and continued success can be attributed to a variety of factors. One factor is the native integration of QR Code readers in smartphone cameras mentioned earlier. Another factor is the specific context of the Covid-19 pandemic. Another factor, which is impossible to quantify but shouldn't be discounted, is that that companies have gotten better at figuring out *when* to use them. Chinese companies were far ahead of most of the West in implementing the symbols efficiently, and Western companies have finally begun to catch up. At least for the near future, it appears that QR Codes are here to stay and will continue to extend barcode technology beyond identification and logistics into new domains.

9 BARCODES AND FIFTY YEARS OF MISPLACED EULOGIES

The fiftieth anniversary of the first UPC barcode will happen on June 26, 2024. The same object that was greeted by protests and Senate hearings in the 1970s will likely begin its fifties with little fanfare. I'm sure some articles will note the event, but most people will have no idea that the barcodes they scan at grocery stores are basically the same barcodes their parents and grandparents scanned decades ago. The fact that the UPC's fiftieth birthday will pass without much notice feels appropriate: maybe the greatest testament to the infrastructural power of the barcode is that they will be scanned billions of times on that June day, and almost no one will give them a second thought.

Barcode technology has continued to evolve in the fifty years since that first UPC barcode was scanned in Troy,

Ohio. More powerful linear barcodes were created; 2D barcodes were invented that could contain significantly more data; QR Codes contributed to new forms of engagement with barcode technology. Despite those changes, barcodes have remained a remarkably consistent object over the last half century. A UPC barcode scanned in a self-checkout line today is, with a few very minor differences, the same object as the very first UPC barcode scanned on a pack of gum in 1974. The line structure is the same; the data standard is almost the same. UPC/EAN barcodes have remained a constant even as everything around them—the scanners, the databases, the computing systems, and on and on—changed significantly. And while the UPC/EAN barcode is the oldest and most recognizable example of the barcode's consistency, other barcode symbols have also endured. Linear barcodes like Code 39 are over forty years old and still widely used. Even many of the 2D barcode symbols discussed in the previous chapter are more than 30 years old. Despite their age, barcodes remain a key data infrastructure that still produces massive amounts of identification data that help hold massive systems together all over the world.

Of course, nothing lasts forever, and some day barcodes will disappear. I have no idea when that day will come, but I am skeptical of predictions that barcodes will be fully replaced any time soon. My skepticism about negative predictions about the barcode's future is rooted in the barcode's past, a past filled with projections that they'd soon be replaced by something "better" and more powerful. As early as the 1970s, people were already writing eulogies for the barcode—and yet they continue to endure as the world's most widely used identification infrastructure. Consequently, this final chapter examines the barcode's possible future by exploring predictions of their imminent demise. I have no idea how long barcodes will remain a key infrastructure in our lives. I do know that, if the past is any indication, they will be far harder to kill off than many people might expect.

Misplaced eulogies

Predictions of the barcode's failure began almost immediately after the UPC was first created. As discussed in chapter 4, the initial rollout of barcodes in US grocery stores was rocky; consumer groups protested, politicians proposed legislation, and many grocery stores were skeptical that barcode systems were worth the large investment. Barely two years after the UPC was formalized, *Business Week* published what was likely the first eulogy for the barcode: a 1976 article called "The Supermarket Scanner That Failed."[1] The tech world is filled with predictions that aged poorly, but it would be difficult to find many articles that aged more poorly than that one. The article still looked fairly solid a few years later, however, when only one percent of grocery stores had installed barcode scanning systems by 1979.[2] Adoption in the late 1970s was so far below industry expectations that some industry executives "lost enthusiasm" for the system and no longer believed it would succeed.[3] People began eulogizing the barcode almost as soon as it was born.

By the early 1980s, rapid increases in barcode adoption showed that worries about the barcode's failure were premature. Despite the successes of the 1980s, however, a new wave of predictions about the barcode's coming obsolescence had already begun. A 1985 *Wall Street Journal* article that documented the barcode's rapid ascendance ended with a section about how "Industry experts predict more efficient technologies will leave bar coding behind over the next two decades."[4] Even a celebration of the barcode's success couldn't help but predict that they were just a placeholder until something better came along.

Linear barcodes then faced their next major threat with the "the two-dimensional tsunami" in the 1990s.[5] Some influential trade publications argued that the supposed 2D sweepstakes would lead to the death of linear barcodes because 2D barcodes were far more powerful. One major industry figure who pushed that view was Craig Harmon, an influential leader in the AIDC industry and one of the foremost experts on barcode technology. In 1994, he wrote an article about the obsolescence of linear barcodes which argued that, "If a single 2-D symbol can record the product code, as well as serial number, lot number, and expiration/freshness date, what is the need for the linear UPC symbol?"[6] Harmon's argument was apparently quite controversial; when I found that article in the George Goldberg archive, someone had written "NAÏVE STATEMENT" in huge letters on the first page. And despite Harmon's expertise, the prediction did end up being somewhat naïve. 2D barcodes have been adopted in some industries, but decades after the supposed "two-dimensional tsunami," they are still far less common than older linear barcodes.

Even as linear barcodes weathered the challenge from their more powerful 2D cousins, another AIDC technology began to be hyped as the barcode's replacement: radio frequency identification (RFID) tags. RFID tags have been around for decades, and they have major advantages over barcodes (whether linear or 2D). For one, the tags can contain exponentially more data, and the major RFID standard—the Electronic Product Code (EPC)—"defines a number range large enough to uniquely identify every object on the planet."[7] Whereas a standard like the UPC identifies a type of item, it does not have the data capacity to differentiate one six-pack of Pepsi from another. RFID tags, on the other hand, can make item identification far more granular. Additionally, whereas barcodes are optical technologies that require a line-of-sight to be read, RFID tags are a wireless technology that can transmit identification data across varying distances depending on the type of tag.[8]

The hype about RFID tags began building in the mid-90s and intensified in 1999 when Kevin Ashton presented a plan for RFID item tagging in supply chains. He first coined the term "Internet of Things" in a an RFID pitch to Proctor & Gamble executives, and the same pitch helped kick off the growing drumbeat that the barcode's days were numbered.[9]

That drumbeat only grew louder in the mid-2000s when Walmart, an early adopter of barcodes, announced a mandate that required suppliers to tag items with RFID.[10] At that point, the RFID hype was at its apex, and barcodes seemed like they might finally be facing a challenger too powerful to endure.

As I'm sure you know if you've bought anything in the last year, the eulogies for the barcode were premature. RFID tags are widely used in some areas, but they have often struggled to gain adoption. Walmart, for example, rolled back their RFID mandate, and other companies shelved plans to shift from barcodes to RFID.[11] RFID tagging certainly hasn't disappeared, but it hasn't reached anywhere near the levels predicted by some of the hype in the mid-2000s. RFID tag usage is still small compared to their less powerful AIDC relative. Barcodes remain exceptionally resilient objects that continue to thrive despite—or maybe because of—their simplicity and limitations.

Barcodes have defied predictions of their demise many times in the previous decades, but a day will eventually come when they are replaced by some other AIDC technology. Maybe RFID will finally live up to its initial hype, or maybe whatever will finally replace the barcode hasn't been invented yet. I have no idea how long barcode systems will remain as one of the most important data infrastructures in the world. But I am sure that barcodes will be difficult to dislodge as the world's most widely used identification infrastructure.

Barcodes have endured and thrived for so long for various reasons. For one, the technology is relatively simple. Data is contained in patterns of lines and spaces, and the data must be structured based upon an established standard. As long as barcodes don't tear and scanners don't break, barcode systems are not particularly complex—especially compared to other AIDC technologies like RFID—and not difficult to train people to use. Much of the barcode's enduring power comes from that simplicity. Barcodes can't contain as much data as other identification technologies, and they have no wireless capabilities. They're a product of the 1970s. But they work well and rarely require more than a fleeting moment of attention.

Maybe the most important reason barcodes continue to thrive doesn't even have much to do with the objects themselves. Barcode systems have defied predictions of their obsolescence in no small part because a massive amount of resources have been invested in barcode systems. As philosopher of technology Langdon Winner argued, once industries settle on a system, "choices tend to become strongly fixed in material equipment, economic investment, and social habit, [and] the original flexibility vanishes for all practical purposes once the initial commitments are made."[12] More industries than I can count have spent huge amounts of money implementing barcode systems. Industries have invested significant time and resources developing detailed barcode data standards. Tens of millions of employees have been trained to scan barcodes in everything from grocery stores to warehouses to delivery vehicles. Even when a better option comes along, moving away from barcodes will require investing many billions of dollars in new systems, countless hours of new employee training, consumer acceptance, and complex industry-wide organization to develop new standards. Whichever AIDC technology eventually replaces the barcode won't just have to be better than the barcode systems we have now; it will have to be *much* better to justify such a massive shift in how so many parts of our world work.

A story partially told

Early in this book I quoted sociologist Nigel Thrift's argument that barcodes were a crucial element in "the new way of the world," yet their story had remained mostly untold. When I started thinking about telling that story, I worried there might not be enough for an entire book. Once I started my research in earnest, I realized the full story of the barcode includes far too much for a single book. I went from initially wondering what to write about to making difficult decisions about which parts of the story I had to cut. For example, I could have included a chapter on the barcode's strangely central role in the history of patent trolls. That story would focus on a man named Jerome Lemelson, who, depending on the source you read, was either one of the greatest inventors of the 20th century or a scam artist and one the most successful patent trolls in history.[13] Lemelson made over

$100 million dollars in the 1990s (based on rulings that were eventually overturned) suing companies because he claimed their barcode systems violated his patents. The sketchy patent practices he used in his barcode lawsuits popularized methods that have been adopted by countless patent trolls in the decades since he made his fortune.

Or I could have included a chapter about the time an activist group tried to go to war with Walmart and used barcodes as their weapon. In 2003, the artist and activist collective The Carbon Defense League launched a project called Re-Code.com. The project invited visitors to "recode your own price" by printing out barcodes for cheaper items and putting them on more expensive items when checking out at Walmart.[14] UPC/EAN barcodes were never designed to be secure and UPC/EAN product numbers aren't private (you can easily look them up on multiple websites).[15] Re-Code.com tried to exploit the barcode system to protest corporate power, and Walmart was not pleased. Walmart sued the project's creators and got the website taken down just a few months after it launched. Re-Code didn't last long, but their attempt to use barcodes—themselves a prominent symbol of capitalism—to throw a wrench in the capitalist system is an interesting tangent in the barcode's larger story. Lemelson's patents and Re-Code's activism are just two examples of the divergences the story could take, a story that could cover all kinds of surprising tangents like failed experiments with "invisible barcodes" and controversies about the use of barcodes in RealID laws.

I didn't briefly mention those examples as a teaser for a future book. I included them to acknowledge that the moments covered throughout these chapters are just one part of a much larger story. Barcodes may seem like they are as mundane an object as one could imagine, and I have certainly gotten some interesting looks when I've told people that I've been writing a book about them. But that mundanity is also their beauty, and their learned invisibility obscures a long history of controversies and conspiracies, successes and failures, and ultimately, resilience. The same barcodes that fed data into massive computers in the 1970s now transmit identification data stored in massive data centers. The same barcodes that were first eulogized in 1976 are scanned billions of times a day in the 2020s. Someday the barcode's story will reach its end, and at fifty years old, the story is likely closer to its end than its beginning. But for the foreseeable future, the barcode's story will continue to be written until they eventually face a challenger they cannot overcome. When that day finally comes, I hope you take a moment to think about what might be the most unexpected part of the story I have told: a committee of grocery executives in the 1970s decided in their final meeting to choose a symbol that eventually became one the most recognizable objects in the entire world.

ACKNOWLEDGEMENTS

I have a soft spot for all my books, but this book has been my passion project. I never would have had either the confidence or the freedom to write such a quirky book if I didn't have so much support in so many parts of my life. The book might only have my name on the cover, but it wouldn't exist without so many people who have helped along the way.

I want to start by thanking Stony Brook University's special collection staff. Fairly early in my research, I luckily found the George Goldberg Collection archive at Stony Brook. The Goldberg Collection is dedicated to preserving primary documents related to barcode history, and I'm not sure how I could have written this book without that archive. In particular, I don't think this book would have been possible without the help of Kristen Nyitray, Stony Brook's Director of Special Collections and University Archives. I had never done research in a physical archive before, and she was amazingly helpful in guiding me through the entire process and arranging for me to spend a week reviewing materials in the early summer of 2022. All of Stony Brook's special collection staff helped me through the process and sat in the room as I read through countless documents, and they could not have been kinder and more welcoming. The inclusion of many of the details in this book would not have been possible without their help. And I also want to thank George Goldberg himself for all the work he put into preserving this important history.

Thanks to my department at Clemson University, particularly my department chair Will Stockton, for being supportive of these strange projects and for funding my archival work. And, of course, I want to thank my family for being supportive in the most important and most general sense. I don't think my Mom or my Dad or my brother ever fully understood just *why* I was so passionate about barcodes, but they supported me nonetheless. I am terrible at answering questions about my work with friends and family, so they've mostly learned not to ask. But regardless, just knowing I have their support whether they know what I'm doing or not means the world to me.

While my department and most of my family supported me in a more general sense, it was my wife Stevie Edwards who gave me the most solid, loving base of support anyone could hope for. Stevie and I got married just 5 months before the Covid-19 lockdowns began, and I don't know how I would have made it through these last 3 years if I didn't have her in my life. I had the time and the confidence to start this project because I knew I would always have her support. She's also the person who had to sit through many random dinner conversations where I would monologue for way too long about some interesting thing I'd just found out about barcodes. She listened every time (or at least did a good job faking it), and she also copyedited the manuscript before I submitted it to publishers. I'm so lucky to have someone in my life who might not quite understand my deep interest in barcodes but was always there to help me through my thoughts.

And finally, I need to thank the group that was maybe the most important to the actual nuts-and-bolts writing process: my three rescue pups Daisy, Tinkerbell, and Peaches. The closest they ever come to engaging with barcodes is when they chew up a package with a barcode label on it, but they snuggled on the couch with me, whined for pets, and demanded walks throughout every step of my writing. Writing is a bit of a lonely process no matter what, but it's a whole lot less lonely when your loving dogs are right there with you as you stare at a blank page.

NOTES

Chapter 1

1 Roman Mars, "Barcodes," *99% Invisible* (podcast), 2014, https://99percentinvisible.org/episode/barcodes/transcript/.

2 Jordan Frith, *A Billion Little Pieces: RFID and Infrastructures of Identification* (Cambridge MA: MIT Press, 2019).

3 GS1, "Barcode 45th Anniversary," Twitter, 2019, https://twitter.com/gs1/status/1143896857531301888?s=20&t=FS9MizhxfBv2Wv6_PGCvEg.

4 Nigel Thrift, *Knowing Capitalism* (London, England: Sage, 2005), 220.

5 "Big data revolutions" comes from Viktor Mayer-Schönberger and Kenneth Cukier, *Big Data: A Revolution That Will Transform How We Live, Work, and Think* (New York, NY: Eamon Dolan/Houghton Mifflin Harcourt, 2013).

6 John T. Dunlop, and Jan Rifkin. "Introduction" in *Revolution at the Checkout Counter*, 1–38. Cambridge MA: Harvard University Press, 1997, 11–13.

7 Weightman, Gavin. "The History of the Bar Code." Smithsonian, 2015. http://www.smithsonianmag.com/innovation/history-bar-code-180956704/.

8   Stephen Brown, *Revolution at the Checkout Counter: The Explosion of the Bar Code* (Cambridge, MA: Harvard University Press, 1997).

9   Nicholas Varchaver, "The Humble Bar Code Began as an Object of Suspicion and Grew into a Cultural Icon," CNNMoney, 2004, https://money.cnn.com/magazines/fortune /fortune_archive/2004/05/31/370719/index.htm.

10 Mars, "Barcodes."

11 "The Supermarket Scanner That Failed," *Business Week*, March 22, 1976.

12 See the appendix of the following book for a collection of more than 270 barcode symbols: Benjamin Nelson, *Punched Cards to Bar Codes* (New York: Helmers Publishing, 1997).

Chapter 2

1   Berry, *The Secret Life of Bar Codes* (London: Wirksworth Books, 2013), 17–20.

2   Ibid., 21.

3   James Beniger, *The Control Revolution* (Cambridge, MA: Harvard University Press, 1986), 411.

4   JoAnne Yates, "Evolving Information Use in Firms, 1850-1920," in *Information Acumen: The Understanding and Use of Knowledge in Modern Business*, ed. Lisa Bud-Frierman (London: Routledge, 1994), 35–36.

5   "Confidential Draft: Choice of a Universal Product Code" (Boston: Harvard Business School, 1974), 2.

6   Leibowitz, Ed. "Bar Codes: Reading between the Lines." *Smithsonian Magazine* 29, no. 11 (1999): 130–45. 132.

7   Joseph Woodland and Bernard Silver, Classifying Apparatus and Method, 2,612,994, filed 1949, and issued 1952, 2.

8   "Confidential Draft: Choice of a Universal Product Code," 1–2.

9   Brown, *Revolution at the Checkout Counter: The Explosion of the Bar Code*, 39.

10 Nelson, *Punched Cards to Bar Codes*, 66.

11 Brown, *Revolution at the Checkout Counter: The Explosion of the Bar Code*, 174–183.

12 "Confidential Draft: Choice of a Universal Product Code," 6.

13 One exception involved figuring out how to get barcodes to work with coupons, which required additional pricing data and was apparently quite the challenge. See Brown, *Revolution at the Checkout Counter: The Explosion of the Bar Code*, 184–193 for more detail.

14 Brown, *Revolution at the Checkout Counter: The Explosion of the Bar Code*, 89.

15 As he explained on an episode of the *99% Invisible* podcast, Laurier strongly believed that the circular codes would not meet the grocery industry's demands, but the issue he faced was that laser scanners at the time mostly used one line to read the code. That meant circular codes tended to work better than horizontal codes. Laurier's solution was to add a second line to the laser scanner, making the X shape still used with barcode scanners to this day. The X could then easily read horizontal codes, so Laurier's contribution came in both the symbol he created and the slight shift in laser scanner technology he pushed for. For more details, see Mars, "Barcodes."

16 Nelson, *Punched Cards to Bar Codes*, 63.

17 Brown, *Revolution at the Checkout Counter: The Explosion of the Bar Code*, 91.

18 John T. Dunlop, and Jan Rifkin. "Introduction," in *Revolution at the Checkout Counter*. Cambridge MA: Harvard University Press, 1997, 19–20.

19 Erick Jones and Christopher Chung, *RFID in Logistics: A Practical Introduction* (New York, NY: CRC Press, 2008), 43.

20 Dunlop and Rifkin. "Introduction," 3.

21 George Goldberg, "Bar Codes Are Here to Stay," *The Journal of the Technical Association of the Pulp and Paper Industry* 64, no. 10 (1984): 1–3.

22 Nelson., *Punched Cards to Bar Codes*, 87–101.

23 Ibid., 99.

Chapter 3

1 GS1, "Barcode 45th Anniversary."

2 Samuel Greengard, *The Internet of Things* (Cambridge, MA: MIT Press, 2015), 10.

3 Hiromi Hosoya and Markus Schaefer, "Bit Structures," in *Harvard Design School Guide to Shopping*, ed. Chuihua Judy Chung et al. (New York, NY: Taschen, 2002), 157.

4 Thrift, *Knowing Capitalism*, 220.

5 Geoffrey C. Bowker "The Infrastructural Imagination" in *Information Infrastructure(s): Boundaries, Ecologies, Multiplicity*, edited by Alessandro Mongili and Giuseppina Pelligrino, xii–xiv. Cambridge Scholars Publishing, 2014, xii.

6 As an extra detail, the line patterns differ on the left and right side of the barcode so that barcodes can be scanned in either direction.

7 This website contains images of each line pattern that can help you decipher barcode lines if you have a lot of extra time on your hands: https://www.101computing.net/upc -barcodes/.

8 Hosoya and Schaefer, "Bit Structures," 157.

9 Rob Kitchin, *The Data Revolution: Big Data, Open Data, Data Infrastructures and Their Consequences* (London, UK: Sage Publications, 2014), 32–36.

10 Susan Leigh Star, "The Ethnography of Infrastructure," *American Behavioral Scientist* 43, no. 3 (November 1, 1999): 380, https://doi.org/10.1177/00027649921955326.

11 Ibid., 380.

12 Christian Sandvig, "The Internet as Infrastructure," in *The Oxford Handbook of Internet Studies*, ed. William H. Dutton, 86–108 (Oxford, UK: Oxford University Press, 2013), 92.

13 "About | GS1," GS1, 2022, https://www.gs1.org/about.

14 A product's UPC/EAN number is publicly available. You can look them up here: https://www.barcodespider.com

15 The "check digit" calculation is a fairly complex mathematical process that is detailed on the following website: https://www .101computing.net/upc-barcode-check-digit-calculation/

16 See Berry, *The Secret Life of Bar Codes* for a more detailed description of how these numbers work.

17 Jordan Frith, *Smartphones as Locative Media* (London, England: Polity Press, 2015), 1–8.

18 John Perry Barlow, "A Declaration of the Independence of Cyberspace," Electronic Frontier Foundation, 1996, https://www.eff.org/cyberspace-independence.

19 Rob Kitchin and Martin Dodge, *Code/Space: Software and Everyday Life* (Cambridge, MA: MIT Press, 2011); de Souza e Silva, "From Cyber to Hybrid: Mobile Technologies as Interfaces of Hybrid Spaces."

20 Some of this bureaucratic work has already been done to plan for the Internet of Things through the creation of IPV6, which massively increases the number of available IP addresses to plan for the huge increase in the number of objects with Internet connections.

Chapter 4

1 "Learned invisibility" comes from Star, "The Ethnography of Infrastructure," 381–382.

2 Brian Larkin, "The Politics and Poetics of Infrastructure," *Annual Review of Anthropology* 42, no. 1, 327–43 (2013): https://doi.org/10.1146/annurev-anthro-092412-155522, 336.

3 "Confidential Draft: Choice of a Universal Product Code." Boston: Harvard Business School, 1974, 8.

4 Brown, *Revolution at the Checkout Counter: The Explosion of the Bar Code*, 125.

5 Ibid., 128.

6 Bernie Lake, "Grocery Robots in Future," *The Salt Lake Tribune*, October 11, 1975, 27.

7 Robbi Goldberg, "The UPC: From Conception to Implementation," 1979, 14.

8   Winifred Cook, "Those Lines Aren't Just Decorations," *The Central New Jersey Home News*, March 30, 1975, A4.

9   This particular quote can be found in the transcript *Symposium on The Universal Product Coding System, Before the Committee on Commerce*, 93rd Congress, 1974.

10 Lake, "Grocery Robots in Future," 27.

11 Cook, "Those Lines Aren't Just Decorations," A4.

12 David Murray, "You'll Never See Price," *The Charlotte News*, March 11, 1975, 8.

13 Don Sellar, "Check-Out Computer Checks-In Problems," *The Calgary Herald*, October 8, 1975, 73.

14 Murray, 8.

15 "Connubial Consumerism," *Wall Street Journal*, August 31, 1976, 10.

16 Joseph Coyle, "Scanning Lights up a Dark World for Grocers," *Fortune*, March 27, 1978, 78.

17 Huyk, Linda. "Michigan Item Pricing Law May Have Changed but Your Consumer Rights Did Not." Michigan State University Extension, 2012. https://www.canr.msu.edu/news/michigan_changed_item_pricing_law_but_your_consumer_rights_did_not.

18 Rose Winters, "Grocery Chains Shelving Computer Checkout Counters," *Lansing State Journal*, October 16, 1978, 13.

19 Susan Moore, "Groups Say Coding System Robs Buyer Knowledge," *Springfield Leader and Press*, September 24, 1975, 34.

20 Nelson, *Punched Cards to Bar Codes*, 66.

21 "Grocers Try Coded Checkouts," *The Manhattan Mercury*, February 10, 1976, 6.

22 *Testimony By Joseph B. Danzansky, President of Giant Food Inc. Before The Maryland Senate Economic Affairs Committee,* 1976.

23 Goldberg, "Bar Codes Are Here to Stay."

24 "Connubial Consumerism," 10.

25 *Testimony By Joseph B. Danzansky*

26 Nigel Thrift, "Remembering the Technological Unconscious by Foregrounding Knowledges of Position," *Environment and Planning D: Society and Space* 22, 175–90 (2004), 181-182.

27 Jim McKay, "Quick Journey Marks Arrival of Just-in-Time Economy," *Pittsburgh Post-Gazette*, August 14, 2005, 27.

28 Robert Rosenblatt and Janice Defao, "Postal Service Plans to Cut 47000 Jobs by 1995," *Los Angeles Times*, September 27, 1991, 1.

29 "Postal Efficiency Could Eliminate 100,000 Jobs," *Lancaster New Era*, September 2, 1991, 27.

30 Ibid.

31 "Postal Automation Cannot Be Held Back," *The Paducah Sun*, November 3, 1990, 4.

32 Rosenblatt and Defao, "Postal Service Plans to Cut 47000 Jobs by 1995," 1.

33 Ibid.

Chapter 5

1 "The Supermarket Scanner That Failed," *Business Week*, March 22, 1976.

2   Goldberg, "Bar Codes Are Here to Stay," 2.

3   "1986 Nielsen Review of Grocery Store Trends," *Progressive Grocer*, September 1986.

4   "56th Annual Report," *Progressive Grocer*, April 1989, 68.

5   "The History of Automatic Identification," *ID Systems* 10 (1991), 1.

6   James Carville and Paul Begala, "It's the Candidate, Stupid!," *New York Times*, December 4, 1992, A34.

7   Andrew Rosenthal, "Bush Encounters the Supermarket, Amazed," *New York Times*, February 4, 1992, A1.

8   Carville and Begala, "It's the Candidate, Stupid!", A34.

9   Michael Pearson, "Five Other U.S. Leaders and the Words That Tripped Them Up," *CNN*, 2014, https://www.cnn.com /2014/08/29/politics/obama-presidential-controversies.

10 Adam Nagourney, "George Bush, Who Steered Nation in Tumultuous Times, Is Dead at 94," *New York Times*, November 30, 2018, A1.

11 "The Reliable Source," *Washington Post*, February 12, 1992, C3.

12 Christopher Cornell, "White House Says Media's Checkout Was Faulty on Scanner Episode," *AP News*, February 11, 1992.

13 Howard Kurtz, "The Story That Just Won't Check-Out," *Washington Post*, February 19, 1992, C1.

14 Jim Hoagland, "Let Bush Be Bush," *Washington Post*, February 5, 1992, A17.

15 Anthony Lewis, "The Two Nations," *New York Times*, February 13, 1992, A27.

16 Mara Leveritt, "Hillary Clinton Talks Back," *Arkansas Times*, August 27, 1992.

17 Linda Qiu, "George Bush's Legacy: Revisiting Past Claims," *New York Times*, December 4, 2018.

18 Ibid.

Chapter 6

1 Revelation, 13: 16-17.

2 Revelation is a notoriously difficult text to interpret, and there are widespread debates about whether it's mean as prophecy or allegory. In addition, there are many interpretations about what the images represent. I did my best to explain briefly explain the book, but you could read someone else and get a very different explanation.

3 Revelation, 13: 1.

4 See the following article for more detail on the contested interpretation of the number of the Beast: M.G. Michael, "Demystifying the Number of the Beast in the Book of Revelation: Examples of Ancient Cryptology and the Interpretation of the '666' Conundrum." *IEEE International Symposium on Technology and Society*, 23–41, 2010.

5 John Englund, "The Mark of the Beast," *Gospel Call*, April 1975.

6 "Prophecy Sunday!," *Lexington Leader*, October 28, 1978, 7.

7 Downs, Albert. "Universal Product Code: The Devil's Work." *The Gazette*, September 15, 1986, 6A.

8 Mary Relfe, *The New Money System* (Ministries, INC, 1982), xxiv.

9 Ibid., 32.

10 Ibid., 37.

11 Ibid., 37.

12 Caroline Drewes, "End-of-the-World Revivalism Became the Stuff of Art," *San Francisco Examiner*, October 20, 1986.

13 Eleanor Dickinson, "Mark of the Beast/Charcoal on Paper (1985)," Eleanor Dickson art, n.d., http://eleanordickinsonart .com/2020/08/18/1985-mark-of-the-beast-charcoal-on-paper -17-x-20-850/.

14 Cade Metz, "Why the Bar Code Will Always Be the Mark of the Beast," *Wired*, 2012, https://www.wired.com/2012/12/upc -mark-of-the-beast/

15 Katherine Albrecht and Liz Mcintyre, *The Spychips Threat: Why Christians Should Resist RFID and Electronic Surveillance* (New York, NY: Thomas Nelson, 2006).

16 Terry L. Cook and Thomas R. Horn, *Beast Tech* (Defender, 2013); Terry L. Cook, *The Mark of the New World Order* (Whitaker House, 1996).

17 Cook and Horn, *Beast Tech*, 99.

18 Metz, "Why the Bar Code Will Always Be the Mark of the Beast."

Chapter 7

1 Mars, "Barcodes."

2 James Cameron, "Terminator Script," Internet Movie Script Database, n.d., https://imsdb.com/scripts/Terminator.html.

3 A few other examples include the 1992 movie *Fortress,* the 1992 movie *The Philadelphia Experiment*, and the 2002 movie *The Island*.

4 Suzanne Weyn, *The Bar Code Tattoo* (Scholastic Paperbacks, 2012).

5 Noam Milgrom-Elcot, "Bar Codes and Tattooed Numbers," Holocaust Visual Archive, 2012, https://holocaustvisual archive.wordpress.com/2012/01/23/bar-codes-and-tattooed -numbers/.

6 Jacqueline Ross, "Identifying Human Trafficking Victims in Health Care," *Journal of PeriAnesthesia Nursing* 35, no. 2, 215–16 (April 1, 2020): https://doi.org/10.1016/j.jopan.2019 .11.006.

7 Kai Hill, "Temporary Tattoos Mark, Target Human Trafficking," University of Miami, 2020, https://news.miami .edu/stories/2020/01/temporary-tattoos-mark-target-human -trafficking.html.

8 Mark Kelner, "Barcodes/The Container," Mark Kelner Portfolio, 2021, https://www.markkelner.com/store.

9 Kelner.

10 "Weekly Art Websites: Barcode Art," *The Independent*, 2011, https://www.independent.co.uk/arts-entertainment/art/ weekly-art-websites-barcode-art-2242903.html.

11 See the following site for a description of how Blake created the piece: Scott Blake, "UPC A/Marilyn Monroe/Movies," Barcode Art, 2011, https://www.barcodeart.com/artwork/ portraits/barcodes/monroe_1.html.

12 Steven McCarthy, "The Art Portrait, the Pixel and the Gene: Micro Construction of Macro Representation," *Convergence* 11, no. 4 (2005): 64.

13 More details on his work can be found at Bernard Solco, "Symbology," Bernard Solco, 2022, https://bernardsolco.com/ barcodes/.

14 The barcodeporn subreddit community can be found at
https://www.reddit.com/r/barcodeporn.

15 Jennifer Donnelly, "Things to Know Before Getting a Barcode
Tattoo," *Tattoodo*, 2020, https://www.tattoodo.com/articles/5
-reasons-why-barcode-tattoos-arent-such-a-great-idea-4815.

16 I tried to sell my partner on the idea, but it did not go well.

Chapter 8

1 Lora Kelley, "Actually, QR Codes Never Went Away," *New
York Times*, January 28, 2021, https://www.nytimes.com/2021
/01/28/style/qr-codes.html.

2 "The History of Automatic Identification."

3 George Goldberg, "The Two-Dimensional Code Sweepstakes,"
Scan Newsletter 13, no. 1 (1989): 7–8.

4 Paul Chartier, "2D Symbologies-A Status Report" (TC225
Working Group 3, 1994).

5 Deb Navas, "2-D Codes' Defining Moment," *ID Systems* 15
(1995), 1.

6 One differentiating feature of QR Codes were that they could
contain Japanese Kanji characters.

7 "Two-Dimensional Codes," *Automatic ID News*, November
1995, 32.

8 Craig Harmon, "Bar Codes Are Dead . . . Long Live 2D!,"
Automatic ID News, October 1996, 22.

9 Leopoldina Fortunati, "The New Frontiers of Mobile Media:
Theoretical Insights on Their Possible Developments," *Living*

inside Mobile Social Information, ed. James Katz (Boston, MA: Greyden Press, 2014), 62.

10 Adam Strout, "The Death Of The QR Code," *Marketing Land*, April 4, 2013, http://marketingland.com/the-death-of-the-qr -code-37902.

11 B.I. Ochman, "QR Codes Are Dead, Trampled by Easier-to- Use Apps," *Ad Age*, 2013, https://adage.com/article/digitalnext /qr-codes-dead-toppled-easy-apps/240548.

12 Scott Stratten, *QR Codes Kill Kittens* (Wiley, 2013).

13 Fortunati, "The New Frontiers of Mobile Media: Theoretical Insights on Their Possible Developments," 64.

14 Kelley, "Actually, QR Codes Never Went Away."

15 Charles Liu, "Sight of Guests Being Advised to Give Cash via Alipay at Beijing Wedding Reception Sparks Backlash," *The Beijinger*, April 26, 2017, https://www.thebeijinger.com/blog /2017/04/25/use-alipay-beijing-wedding-reception-sparks -backlash.

16 Phillip Pantuso, "The Second Life of the QR Code," *PR Week*, March 31, 2022, https://www.prweek.com/article/1751383 ?utm_source=website&utm_medium=social.

17 Jamie Cohen, "2021 Was the Year of the QR Code," *Debugger*, December 31, 2021, https://debugger.medium.com/an-ode-to -the-code-2021-is-the-year-of-the-qr-code-dfe90639ee17.

Chapter 9

1 "The Supermarket Scanner That Failed."

2 Richard A. Rauch, "The Universal Produce Code and Computer Assisted Scanning: A Marketing Case Study," PhD diss., (New York University, 1979).

3 Winters, "Grocery Chains Shelving Computer Checkout Counters," 13.

4 Linda Watkins, "Bar Codes Are Black-and-White Stripes and Soon They Will Be Read All Over," *Wall Street Journal*, January 8, 1985, 39.

5 Russ Adams, "Two-Dimensional Tsunami," *Automatic ID News*, May 1998, 28.

6 Craig Harmon, "Two-Dimensional Systems and ISO Update," *ID Systems*, November 1994, 22.

7 Rob Kitchin and Martin Dodge, "Barcodes and RFIDs," in *Globalization in Practice*, ed. Nigel Thrift (Oxford University Press, 2014), 270.

8 Frith, *A Billion Little Pieces: RFID and Infrastructures of Identification*, 65-68.

9 Ibid, 51-53.

10 Bob Violino, "Wal-Mart Expands RFID Mandate," *RFID Journal*, 2003, http://www.rfidjournal.com/articles/view?539.

11 Matthew Malone, "Did Wal-Mart Love RFID to Death?," *ZDNet*, 2012, http://www.zdnet.com/article/did-wal-mart-love-rfid-to-death/.

12 Langdon Winner, *The Whale and the Reactor : A Search for Limits in an Age of High Technology* (Chicago: University of Chicago Press, 1986), 29.

13 Michael Kernan, "Around the Mall and Beyond," *Smithsonian Magazine*, July 1996; Bernard Wysocki Jr., "How Patent Lawsuits Made a Quiet Engineer Rich and Controversial," *The Wall Street Journal*, April 9, 1997.

14 Mieszkowski, Katherine. "Steal This Barcode." *Salon*, 2003. https://www.salon.com/2003/04/10/barcode/.

15 One example is the site Barcode Lookup: https://www.barcodelookup.com/

INDEX